No Body's PERfecT

Stories by Teens About Body Image, Self-Acceptance, and the Search for Identity

Kimberly Kirberger

Scholastic Inc.

New York Toronto London Auckland Sydney
Mexico City New Delhi Hong Kong Buenos Aires

With love I dedicate this book to:
My son, Jesse, who is my inspiration, and
Alexander Witt, who taught me
the importance of loving myself

No part of this publication may be reproduced in whole or in part, or stored in a retrieval system, or transmitted in any form or by any means, electronic, mechanical, photocopying, recording, or otherwise, without written permission of the publisher. For information regarding permission, write to Scholastic Inc., Attention: Permissions Department, 557 Broadway, New York, NY 10012.

ISBN 0-439-42638-3

Text copyright © 2003 by Kimberly Kirberger. All rights reserved. Published by Scholastic, Inc. SCHOLASTIC and associated logos are trademarks and/or registered trademarks of Scholastic, Inc.

12 11 10 9 8 7 6 5 4   4 5 6 7 8/0

Design by Steve Scott

Printed in the United States   23

First printing, February 2003

Contents

Acknowledgments

With Gratitude and Appreciation

I thank God for the blessing of this book and all the people that made it happen. I wish to first thank my son, Jesse, because he continually makes me want to be a better person. And not just because he is my son but also because he is someone I look up to and someone who deserves the best. I love you with all my heart.

There were many teenagers who were involved in this book. They read, they suggested, they guided, and they shared. This book comes to you from their hearts and their generosity: Christine Kalinowski, Brie Gorlitsky, Hayley Gibson, Jenny Sharaf, Lindsey Owens, Taylor Fisher, Ashley Fisher, Gina Assadi, Kelly Winters, Caitlen Owens, and Rebecca.

Tasha Boucher, my senior editor and dear friend, not only gave her heart and soul and countless hours to this book, she also shared her brilliance and her love for teenagers. Many times she took my jumbled thoughts and made sense out of them. She helped to organize the book by suggesting that the 24 steps be used to introduce each chapter. This alone was a great gift. Once the format was established, it was (almost) smooth sailing from there.

Mitch Claspy's title is vice president of I.A.M. for Teens, Inc., but his contribution is so much more than that. His work ethic, his attention to detail, and his loyalty are immeasurable. I don't even know how to properly thank him here. Let me just say, I can't imagine having done this book without him. Besides that, I love him dearly.

Lisa Vazquez is a shining light in my day. She helps me with just about everything and does it with a smile. I admire her positive attitude, her professional abilities, and her incredible patience with me. She has acted as administrative coordinator, personal assistant, jewelry designer, stylist, and special projects vice president.

I give my deepest thanks and love to my wonderful brother Jack, who made all of this possible and who continues to be my mentor and hero.

Tasha, Mitch, Lisa, Christine, and Brie have all been called on to be my therapists and best friends more times then I want to admit. I cannot thank them enough for putting up with me while I was doing this book. Let's just say that when I took on the responsibility of writing about self-acceptance, I had to come face-to-face with my own lack of it. I can now honestly say that working on this book has been the most amazing learning experience I have ever had, and I know firsthand that these steps work. However, my dear coworkers had to put up with many tears and listen to many hours of my drama. I only pray that I can pay them back with my friendship.

Lia Gay is, in many ways, the reason I began working with teenagers. When she was a teen, we became good friends and have remained so ever since. She is an amazing writer, a courageous human being, and someone for whom my love is unconditional. The way I feel about her is no different than it would be if she were my child. Lia, I love you and I know you feel good about all the progress you have made on your journey toward self-acceptance.

Christine Kalinowski is one of two teenagers who was involved with this book every step of the way. She read hundreds of stories and chose those that were the best. She gave me feedback on my words and thoughts and how I presented them to you. She gave me inspiration, ideas, and total dedication to this project. She is also my dear friend and a constant reminder of why I love working for and with teenagers so much.

Brie Gorlitsky is the other teenager who was hands-on throughout this entire project. She read everything numerous times and gave me constructive feedback on how to make it better. She always showed up just when I needed her, whether it was during the week or on weekends. It seemed like she was somehow connected to me and this project in a way that was deeper than schedules and work hours. Her support ranged from editorial assistance to bunny care. All of it was of equal importance and I am very grateful to have her in my life.

Hayley Gibson and Jenny Sharaf were also huge participants in this book. They read thousands of stories (literally), did Internet research, and tirelessly searched for stories by teens that would inspire and support you. They also receive the letters and e-mails that teens send to us and make sure that every one of them is read. They often respond to letters personally because they feel that the sender needs some extra love and support. I am so honored that these teens are part of my staff, and I love them lots.

Bonnie Solow is by far the best agent a writer could ever have. She has supported me in ways that go above and beyond what is expected, and her ability to do every aspect of her job brilliantly is nothing short of amazing. I honestly feel that any words I could write would be trite in comparison with how I feel. My heart is so full of love and gratitude for her, and I am continually humbled that I have been blessed to work with such a fine human being.

I want to say a very special thank-you to Joy Peskin, my editor at Scholastic. It is a generous thing to work very hard to make someone else's writing look good. In truth, I am an advocate for teens and someone who has dedicated her life to making teens' lives better, but I am not a writer. Joy was able to perform magic with what I put down on paper. She has been patient and kind, and I appreciate her more than words can say. She, of course, could have said this much better.

I want to thank my editorial director at Scholastic, Craig Walker, for giving this project his enthusiasm from day one. I can safely say that he is a big reason this book happened. How do you thank someone for that?

From the bottom of my heart I want to thank Jean Feiwel, my publisher at Scholastic, for believing in this project and for caring so much about teenagers and all young people. You have been a constant source of inspiration for me while writing this book.

I want to thank Peter Vegso, my publisher at Health Communications, for his continued support and friendship. Peter is completely dedicated to publishing books that help others, and he has an extra-special place in his heart for teenagers. Because of this shared love for teens and because of his sincere kindness, he has my respect and my gratitude.

I want to thank Steven Marshank for his brilliant contributions to this book and for all the managerial expertise that he generously shared with me throughout this process. I also want to thank him for his friendship and for being there for me at a time when I really needed it.

Last, but by no means least, I want to thank my dear friend Colin Mortensen. I always struggle with what to say when thanking him because he has given so much in so many different ways. He is a great supporter of teens, and he is dedicated to giving them healthier messages about their bodies and their behavior. He is a mentor to my son, enriching his life and teaching him many positive things. He is my partner in working with and for teens, and he is one of the good guys.

I am filled with gratitude and I have no question that I could not have done this book without all the people mentioned, and many who have not been. I am realizing as I write this that if I were to properly thank everyone who deserves it, these acknowledgments would be far too long.

Introduction

I have received countless letters from teens who are dealing with eating disorders and weight problems. Many who write to me are lost and frightened in their search for identity. Some have written about their inability to tell someone about a problem they are having. They want to ask for help, but they don't know where to turn. Some have told me they feel unlovable because they consider themselves overweight or unattractive. Each letter made me want to do something to help. I desperately wanted to offer whatever support I could.

I began to collect stories and poems by teens who were dealing with body image issues, and I started doing research on the subject. I talked to teens about their feelings and experiences, and I began to realize that although body image was the obvious problem, the bigger issue — and the one that seemed to be at the root of each letter — was a lack of self-love. I began to examine other problems that teens struggle with — depression, self-mutilation, drug and alcohol addiction, suicide — and I saw a common thread that ran through all of them. It is my belief that the basis of these and other related problems is a lack of self-love and self-acceptance. I realized that, like so many adults, teenagers are not giving themselves the love and acceptance they so desperately need to live healthy, happy lives.

Although this book couldn't possibly contain the solutions to all of the problems you may be struggling with, it is a very good place to start. If you are facing any of the more serious issues written about in this book — if you think you might have an eating disorder, if you are cutting or otherwise hurting yourself, if you think you may have a problem with addiction — it is absolutely imperative that you tell an adult as soon as possible in order to get the help you need. As you will find in reading these stories, there is no shame in asking for help when you need it. In fact, doing so takes great courage.

In the two years I spent working on this book, I thought a lot about how I have gotten through rough times in the past. I wrote down things I have learned from reading books, attending various seminars, and simply living life. I spoke to teenagers and asked if they had any advice or coping techniques. The more teens I spoke to, the more I realized that there are certain common ways we all have for helping ourselves through hard times. Though they weren't always expressed in exactly the same way, the general methods of coping were similar. I decided to arrange these techniques into steps. I had more meetings with teens and spent countless hours with two of the teens on my staff and with my senior editor, Tasha. What we came up with were 24 steps you can use to achieve a more balanced and happy life. I would recommend reading the first chapter in this book, "Get to Know Yourself," first, but you don't have to master step number one before you can move on to step number two. It is my most sincere belief that if you focus each day on just one of these steps — whichever you choose — your life will begin to change for the better.

Once you read and begin practicing these steps, you may see that much of this is advice you have already heard and will continue to hear time and time again. The wording and the context in which it is being offered may be different, but the basic ideas are the same. This was my intent. The best guidelines for life are always the simplest ones. The advice you hear over and over again tends to be the most useful. So many of these wise words have become clichés, which makes them hard to take seriously. Try not to let that stand in your way. Statements such as "stay true to yourself," and "look within" are in fact useful and very profound. You may never have taken the time to think about what they *really* mean. Now you will.

The goal of this book is to help you change the way you look at yourself and, more important, the way you treat yourself. The stories I have compiled are written by teenagers just like you. Many will have something in them that you can relate to. You will learn from the writers' experiences. You will see that you are not alone.

The journey of self-discovery and self-love is one filled with great happiness and sometimes great sorrow. As you start to work with the 24 steps, you will see that joy cannot exist without pain and struggle. Learning to love yourself has to begin with the realization that sometimes you don't. Try not to judge yourself or get frustrated when you're dealing with difficult thoughts or emotions. Instead, remember that you are getting to know yourself in a deeper, more meaningful way. You are making changes now that many people go through an entire lifetime not even knowing need to be made.

I hope that you will get whatever it is you need from this

book. The teens who wrote the stories and poems you are about to read shared a very deep and vulnerable piece of themselves. They did so as a gift to you, so that you could learn from their pain and share in their healing.

The 24 steps in this book are designed to suggest goals and to give you some guidance in achieving them. All you need to get going is the desire to change the way you treat yourself and the way you perceive the world around you. Starting today, you will begin to understand that you already possess the love you want and need.

It's inside of you.

No Figure in My Utopian World

In my utopian world
there would be no perfect figure.
Young women wouldn't strive
to look like one another.
Young souls wouldn't shatter
in disappointment to look
like the thin.
Beauty would only be found
from within.
Supermodels in our society would be the Mother Teresa types,
so loving, beautiful, and gifted
inside.
Too fat . . .
Too thin . . .
Too short . . .
Too tall . . .
It's all a game,
a game that we no longer
have to play.
If we lived in my utopian world
human figures would be
the last talk of the day.

Wearing a bathing suit wouldn't
be as hard as it is.
Young girls wouldn't harm
their bodies to please their peers.
If we lived in my utopian world.
There would be
no perfect figure
only perfect love.

Bianca Gamble

Get to Know Yourself

I want to know what sustains you from the inside
when all else falls away.
I want to know if you can be alone with yourself,
and if you truly like the company you keep in the empty moments.

Oriah Mountain Dreamer

Get to Know Yourself

When we begin to consciously observe ourselves and contemplate the question "Who am I?" we realize that we are multifaceted — unique in many ways and also very much alike.

I went for a walk recently. My destination was the top of a mountain with a breathtaking view. When I got there, I looked out in one direction and saw rolling hills, trees, blue sky, and beautiful boulders. Then I turned slightly to the left and the view was completely different. I saw a small city with houses, backyards, and an occasional swimming pool. As I started to turn again, I quickly realized that I was about to take in another completely new and different view. That is when it struck me that life is the same as the view from a mountaintop. It all depends on how we look at it.

When getting to know ourselves, we often look from only one direction. Many of us look from the direction that sees only shortcomings and flaws. Some of the negative qualities we perceive in ourselves have some basis in reality. But if that is all we are looking at, we are missing the full picture.

It is important to take the time to get to know all of you. Look at your physical, emotional, intellectual, and spiritual attributes. Figure out what is important to you and what makes you happy. Examine with great attention what you love and what you dislike. Determine what is most important to you and what you really don't care much about. Look at these things objectively, without judgment. Leave no stone unturned as you get to know yourself and learn what makes you the wonderfully, uniquely special person that you are.

My Moment of Truth

Hi, my name is Candice and I'm fat. No, you did not just walk into an Overeaters Anonymous meeting. I just wanted to get that out, right away. Some people might think it's not politically correct to use such a vulgar term. They'd prefer I call myself some nice euphemism like cherubic, voluptuous, or for those lovers of *Xena, Warrior Princess,* Amazonian. However, when you are thirteen years old, stand five feet tall on tippy-toes, and weigh in at 150 pounds, most kids your age don't express your condition in such tender terms. I have been called such names as Lardo, Wide Load, and even, "Candy, the Candy Terminator, No Candy Is Safe with Her Around."

Ironic, isn't it, that my parents named me after my own Achilles heel . . . food? But an ice cream sundae is no substitute for a social life. Not even when they give you extra sprinkles. There is simply not enough ice cream in the world that could make me impenetrable to the hurtful things kids say about me.

I have always enjoyed the movies. It is a way of buying a ticket to the ultimate escape. Movies are a common thread running through most of my memories. Like the summer my parents sent me to a camp for overweight kids in upstate New York. I hated it. Being raised in New York City, I preferred sterile concrete to tick-infested woods. The only nights I ever looked for-

11

ward to were movie nights in the old casino house. The spray of light from the old projector mesmerized mosquitoes from across the Catskills. There was always that one rebel mosquito that was strangely attracted to the images on the old, worn-out movie screen. It would dance across the scenes; sometimes it was a mustache, sometimes a beard, sometimes it appeared as a kind of weird growth on an actor's nose. I felt like that lone insect in my own life. I was in the picture, and yet no one in the scene seemed to notice me.

That is what I remember most about my time at Camp Stanley. That, and the way we sat around at night discussing Chips Ahoy, Entenmann's, and Frito Lay as if they were friends back home we longed to see. And, for some, these were indeed their only friends.

I was a chubby toddler and progressed through life expanding ever larger. My size did not go unnoticed by my peers. You would think I would have grown tougher from the years of name-calling. You would be wrong. I enacted the classically wrong reaction every time: I cried. And I cried easily.

My mother would try to console me after school each day. She would lecture me, like a pathetic old football coach trying to boost the morale of his losing team. "They are just jealous of you, honey," she'd recite regularly. "Just ig*nore* them!"

But I knew that she was lying to me. I knew that the whole entire school, including the janitorial staff, could not be jealous of me. Yes, even the school janitor had commented about my size.

My free-flowing tears only loaded my enemies' guns with powerful ammunition. Each of their shots hit the mark. Their constant taunts made me less than excited to go to school with each passing day. I was never going to be acceptable to them and as a result, my self-esteem was becoming nonexistent.

One day, I was watching *Oprah*. She had this show on called "Fighting Back." There was this middle-aged guy on the panel. He was obviously losing his hair. He had this black fringe of hair around the back of his head. Then, way, way up on top, only a few lonely hairs remained. They were like the lone survivors on a desert island. The man, in an effort to conceal his baldness, let his last two precious hairs grow quite long. With his comb, he could swirl them around his head like a cinnamon bun. He reminded me of a friend of my dad's who swam at our community pool. Whenever he stepped out of the water, his long top hairs would flop over to the side of his head. The wet strands of hair congealed together and appeared as some sort of lovestruck sea urchin, nibbling amorously at the poor man's sunburnt ear. His bald head gleamed in the white-hot sun like an SOS. It was quickly noticed by all the neighborhood kids, who would laugh at his expense. But the bald man never seemed to care. He'd just carefully smooth the hairs back into place, suck in his gut, and step out of the troubled waters. Maybe he didn't notice those kids and their cruelty. Maybe he didn't care. Maybe he was in denial. Denial must be like a kind of Disneyland for the adult mind. However, I digress. The man on *Oprah* did not deal as well with the criticism he received from his coworkers. He admitted that he had never fought back. He grew those few sad hairs longer, as if he could hide beneath them.

Oprah told him that he had to come out from hiding behind his hairs, that he was a smart man with a lot to offer the world.

13

He should not let these bullies stand in his way. He must confront them. They did not dictate who he was in life.

"You," she told him, "are the only one who is in control of your destiny!"

The whole audience cheered for Oprah. They cheered for the balding man. But most of all, they cheered for the free foot massager and bunion remover they would receive after the show.

Was I like the balding man? Was I eating my way into hiding? My weight, like his hair, was something I could never hide behind. It was that day that I decided to fight back.

The next day in school my science teacher, Mr. Roster, was leading the class in a lab. Of course Jill and Haley, the popular girls, were chatting up a storm. Mr. Roster looked up quite suddenly. He was annoyed at their disturbance.

"Would you girls like to share what you are chatting about with the class?" asked Mr. Roster.

The whole class turned to watch what would happen next. They were like rubberneckers around a three-car pileup. I also turned to look. Bad move on my part. Haley's eyes hit mine like a dart hitting its target.

"What are you looking at, Chubbo? Time for another feeding at the zoo?"

Now the whole class turned its eyes on me. As I turned and looked back at the smirking faces, something finally hit me. Maybe it was Oprah and the bald man. Maybe it was all those years of abuse, which had struck a final chord inside my soul. Or maybe it was just the heartburn I felt from the tuna tortillas they had served for lunch that day in the cafeteria. It doesn't matter. Whatever it was, it was *my* moment of truth. I would not look away. I would not cry. I was in control of my destiny. I would confront my fears. With fire in my eyes and total conviction on my side, I looked Haley and all the others who had ever hurt me in my life straight in the eyes and said, "Maybe your little friends aren't afraid of you . . . but I am!"

Of course right away I knew I had said the wrong thing. What I meant to say was, "Maybe your little friends *are* afraid of you . . . but I'm *not!*"

Well, it seems it didn't matter what I said that day. The point is, I stuck up for myself. I didn't run away. Haley and her friends never bothered me again. Maybe it was because they saw the fire in my eyes, or maybe it was because they thought I was totally insane. It just doesn't matter. The important thing is that I confronted my fears and I was still standing.

That was the day I felt like I was no longer watching the world from the outside looking in. I was no longer that dull mosquito thrashing wildly against the movie screen. I was in this movie now, and I liked the ending.

C. S. Dweck

E Unum Pluribus

She's an artist of sorts,
With her brushes and paints.
But she doesn't use canvas,
It's opinion she taints.

Around certain "friends"
She paints on a grin,
So she can be popular,
So she can fit in.

With other friends,
She's loud and obscene.
It's the aim of the game,
To be rowdy and mean.

Close to her family,
She's quiet and shy.
They hardly take notice
If she is nearby.

When she's with the guys,
She's a tease and a flirt.

She gives and she gives,
Ignoring the hurt.

The people nearby her,
They hope and they pray
That they could be popular,
Like her one day.

But when she's alone,
She breaks down and cries.
For there is no answer,
When she asks, "Who am I?"

Sara Guilliam

This Is Who I Am

As I lay awake at night,
I think about the day that just went by,
Wondering if I could have changed anything to make it better.

I think about my future,
What I can do to reach my dreams,
How to achieve them,
If I have what it takes,
And if I'm on the right path in life.

I think about my past,
All the people I've met,
Who I've liked and disliked,
My family and friends,
How I grew up,
And what I've accomplished.

I think about what's really important to me,
My morals and values.

I think of how the world works,
And how I would change it if I could.

I think of what I've been through,
And how I feel.

At the end of the day
I think about who I am.

Eva Doty

Stay True to Yourself

*Happiness is when what you think, what you say,
and what you do are in harmony.*

Mahatma Gandhi

Stay True to Yourself

Your truth comes from inside of you and it usually speaks in a quiet, soft voice. This inner voice does not judge or condemn you; it just tells it like it is. Loving yourself means listening to that voice and honoring it.

Have you ever done something you had a bad feeling about at the time and then later found yourself thinking, *I knew I shouldn't have done that?* When you don't listen to your inner voice, you can do things you may later regret. Your inner voice is your compass. It reminds you to stay on course, to be true to yourself, and do what feels right to you.

Sometimes it is difficult to stay true to yourself. You resolve to save money for something important, then you find yourself going to the mall with friends and spending more than you had intended. Or you decide you want to take time one weekend to catch up on your homework, then you find yourself agreeing to baby-sit. There are certainly bigger mistakes you can make. Sadly, you can end up paying in serious ways for not listening to your inner voice.

Sometimes it takes tremendous willpower to honor your commitments to yourself. But your inner voice knows you very well. When you listen to it and take actions that honor it, you usually make good choices.

Pay attention to your inner voice. Love yourself enough to stay true to yourself.

Putting All My Eggs in One Basket

The summer I wrote my novel was one of the happiest times in my life. But all my boyfriend had to say about it was: "You put all your eggs in one basket this summer." He gripped the steering wheel, and his eyes looked straight ahead. I felt blindsided the way I always did when he criticized me. Like the time he said I should dye my hair blond.

"You spent your whole summer writing that book," he added. "You should've gotten a summer job." I hadn't needed a summer job — though I'd had one the previous summer. I lived at home; my parents gave me a small allowance.

All my eggs in one basket. Why did he say that to me? In August, when I'd told him I was already on the second to last chapter, he'd said, "It's great that it seems to come so easily." And now he was begrudging me my happy, productive summer.

That summer I learned the discipline required to become a novelist. Most weekdays I woke around nine, showered, and sat at the kitchen table with a bowl of cereal, a cup of sweetened Lipton's tea, and *The Journals of Sylvia Plath*. I'd eat and read, eating Plath's determination to be a writer, eating the books by writers she read — Virginia Woolf and D. H. Lawrence and dozens of others — her plans to study languages; her work on poems and short stories; her bitter, slangy talk; her jealousy of

25

other writers' successes; her stormy relationship with her husband, Ted Hughes; always her love of words, of books.

Then I'd go in my room and lie on my bed with a spiral notebook and a pen. I'd make sketchy outlines of what would happen in each chapter, but the writing flowed. The novel was about my girlfriends and me, my first nightclub rock 'n' roll shows, my first kiss, our adventures, romantic experiences, friendships and conflicts, crushes and loves. Sometimes it was fun, reliving times with my old friends. Sometimes I'd get bored with the whole thing. But I kept on.

I loved telling stories, even before I could write. My dad, a screenwriter, had encouraged me. He taped me telling little stories into his tape recorder. Later I scribbled stories and poems, kept a journal, and even wrote a novel about the romance between a thirty-four-year-old Englishman and a sixteen-year-old girl whom he'd kidnapped. I would bring the latest installment to school, and my friend Amanda would sit on the hall carpet and read it, spellbound, like it was the latest episode of *General Hospital*. Then she'd demand: "And then what happened?" Eventually I finished that book and, with my mom's help, sent it to publishers. None of them had shared Amanda's enthusiasm.

But this summer seemed different, my days structured around writing. I had found my center. I felt I was backed up by all the writers before me, that they were supporting me and egging me on. I was a writer.

What could I say to my boyfriend that day in his car? I don't remember saying anything, except perhaps that I didn't need a job. I was stunned by his words. All my eggs in one basket — the implication was that if my new novel didn't get published, my summer would've been wasted. I couldn't explain it to him: That this is the best possible way I could've spent the summer.

Writing may not have kept Sylvia Plath sane, but I knew writing was good for my mental health. I was still a teenager, while my boyfriend was in his early twenties and worked full-time. Did I get that he was threatened by my solid sense of myself? And jealous of the fact I had parents who encouraged me, unlike his parents, who hadn't even pushed him to go to college?

He was older, so it was hard for me to see where he was coming from or to notice him trying to chip away at me, to knock me down a few pegs so he could feel better about himself. It didn't occur to me that his comments might mean he wasn't the right guy for me. His words hurt me, but I kept working on my novel. Much later, some sections from it did get published in a magazine, but that wasn't the point. What mattered was that I knew who I was, and what I loved to do. And no one could take that away from me.

Gwynne Garfinkle

One Chance to Be Me

Today for a second I waited,
A pause that I needed to take.
Held tight were my eyes to the pillow,
Delayed was the motion to wake.
A moment was needed to listen,
To the silence that filled the new day.
A moment to be more decisive,
About the self that I want to portray.

Sometimes I wish I felt pretty.
Sometimes I wish I was more.
Sometimes I wish I could vanish,
Through a promising wide-open door.
Sometimes I wish I felt needed.
Sometimes I wish it was true.
Sometimes I wish I could realize,
All the things that I've needed to do.

But the wishes of maybe are countless,
And the hours do not disagree,
That time makes a habit of slipping away
And there's only one chance to be me.

I'll always know when I'm tired,
And I'll always know each mistake.
I'll always know when I'm happy,
And I'll always know when I'm fake.
I'll never regret that which happens,
I'll never deny a good friend.
I'll never, on purpose, harm my own heart,
I'll be there for *me* in the end.

Alison Dankmeyer

365 Days

I was popular for exactly one year. All through eighth grade, to be exact. The irony of my popularity was lost on no one, particularly me; after all, I had spent the first few years of middle school labeled as a complete dork, among other not-so-nice things. How was I instantaneously catapulted from the crowd everyone tried to avoid to the crowd everyone wanted to be in? There was only one explanation: fate.

The first day of gym class that year we all sat around on the dusty floor listening to guidelines for the dress code, the rules of good sportsmanship, and the expectation of enthusiastic participation. (Yeah, right.) I fell into a bit of a daze as our teacher droned on and on, until she stated that it was time to assign locker partners. Everyone began glancing around covertly at the girls sitting around them, wondering whose smelly socks would be next to their own for the next ten months.

She read off the pairs, one by one. They were randomly picked, and therefore no one could accurately predict how much they might suffer from the results. When the gym teacher read my name, I closed my eyes and waited. The name that followed was that of the most popular girl in my grade. My stomach dropped. I would have rather been assigned to the most unhygienic of partners than someone so pretty, so well liked — and who was such a snob. She turned around and glared at me, clearly expressing her own disgust with the cruel hand destiny had dealt her. I sighed heavily, anticipating that this year would be no easier than the last.

But I was wrong. The fact was that although I wasn't stylish, I was kind, and although I was not gorgeous, I had a good sense of humor. And contrary to my own first impressions, my partner was actually quite intelligent and fun to be around. As a result, the very stifled conversations she and I shared for the first few weeks ("Are these your socks or mine?") slowly developed into discussions on the pointlessness of floor hockey, what the cafeteria food was *really* made of, and whether our English teacher was actually crazy or just trying to keep us interested in her lectures.

As different as night and day, the two of us somehow became close. Thus, I became popular by association. From that point on, I never spent a single song against the wall at dances, and I was at the mall every weekend. Though I didn't make the cheerleading squad (I still maintain the auditions were rigged — I could cartwheel with the very best of them), I spent each football game in the stands surrounded by people who had never seemed to notice me before. I had gone from being virtually invisible to someone people wanted to be seen with — in a matter of weeks.

Undoubtedly, popularity had its benefits. It was a relief not to be called names anymore, and it was a comfort to feel as though I belonged. The year flew by instead of dragging on forever, and soon we had graduated, spent a summer at the pool, and were starting our freshman year of high school.

I walked in with my friend at my side, certain that we were

automatically in. What I found, however, was that with many more students, there came many more groups and cliques who were just as popular as ours. People did not necessarily accept you just because you were admired in middle school. As the first weeks went by, I found myself struggling to keep up and doing things I didn't feel comfortable doing in order to keep my social status. It didn't take me long to realize that the social scene was no longer for me, so one day I did the unthinkable: I sat at a different table for lunch.

The people I sat with that day became dear friends for the next four years, and are still my friends today. They liked me simply because of who I was, not because I could get them invited to parties or introduce them to the hottest guys. I always felt comfortable with them, and their support encouraged me to broaden my horizons. Instead of cheerleading, we joined the choir. Instead of hanging out at the mall, we planned picnics in the park.

Their admiration was sincere and reciprocated.

365 days of popularity had taught me to recognize what was artificial and fake. Years of being "just another girl" taught me that true friendship is found in unlikely places and that sincerity beats popularity hands down. It is better to be complimented on your kindness than your clothes. It is more gratifying to be admired for your talents than your status. Accepting yourself as you are, and finding friends who love you because you *are* that person, will provide more happiness and comfort than any amount of popularity ever could.

Kelly Garnett

Lost in a Sea of Faces

My senior year I was crowned Homecoming Queen, an honor given to me by my friends and peers. As the banner rolled down the side of the gymnasium with my name written in huge block letters, my vision blurred and my past surfaced. The sea of faces cheering in the stands faded away, and I was left alone with my past.

It was sixth grade promotion, the biggest transition I had faced, and I shook in my new white high heels. I was awkward in elementary school, harassed for my buckteeth and flat chest, tormented by the boys for being ugly, and mocked by the girls for being meek. All I ever wanted was to be accepted. And as I stood there looking out at all of the familiar faces, I wondered if I ever would be.

The following summer was one of extreme growth for me. I grew into my awkward self, finding a voice and a new release: writing. I had kept a journal for years before, but only now had I made it a daily routine. I expressed my fears, doubts, worries, and dreams in my denim-covered notebook — through poetry, through prose, and through everyday ideas. Through writing, I found a friend — myself.

On the first day of junior high, I stared into the bathroom

mirror at home. "All right, Becca," I said. "Whatever happens, happens. Don't be afraid." I smiled to myself, kissed my mom good-bye, and scurried to the bus stop. That first day of school was inspiring. I had a great schedule with nice teachers, and I made plenty of new acquaintances. As the year progressed, my number of friends increased and my awkward appearance melted away. I no longer spent lunch in the bathroom or did all of my assignments alone. The boys who made fun of me a year ago were now asking me to the movies, and the girls who had once ignored me were sitting with me at lunch. I was accepted. The years passed.

I was popular and therefore stuck with an image I didn't quite know how to handle. I hid every flaw, every feeling, and every insecurity behind makeup and smiles that weren't real. I didn't understand why I felt so unhappy. Popularity wasn't supposed to be lonely.

I wrote more and more, hiding my pain and confusion in the pages of my journal. I didn't want my peers to know that I was human, and therefore I didn't open up to anyone. My true colors were deep within me, scribbled in the darkness of my soul. I forgot how it felt to be on the other side, so when my friends would ridicule and make fun of others, I stood back in disregard. I became one of the girls who used to make me cry, and yet I didn't want to break away. I depended on my friends and not myself. I didn't want to be my own best friend, because then I might lose my place, my identity. I didn't understand that I already had both.

I spoke at our junior high graduation, preparing the class for a new change: high school. As I stood before my friends and acquaintances, I welled up with tears. I didn't like the girl I had become. I was lost.

High school was the same. I still stuck by my friends, but I knew I needed to find myself. I watched my friends struggle with their own identities. I watched them hide behind the same smiles. I watched them ridicule and mock, in spite of their own insecurities and confusion. And finally I had enough. One day at lunch I broke down.

Lunch was a time for gossip and discussion. Who was dating whom and who was wearing what. I was at the point where I didn't really care, and so that day I ate my lunch without the usual commentary. "Becca, what's your deal?" Monica asked.

"My *deal*?" That was it; I backlashed. I began yelling hysterically. I told them all how sick I was of all the talk, the walk, the image. I told them that I wanted to be real, that I was confused, just like everybody else. I told them about elementary school, and how I would come home every day crying, because I wasn't accepted, because I wasn't good enough. I told them that I hurt and felt like I wasn't supposed to, and that I wrote poetry and hid it in fear of revealing part of me that no one knew existed. I opened up every pore and detoxed right there in the middle of lunch.

Silence. No one knew what to say. It didn't matter; they didn't need to say anything. They felt the same as I did, they were just afraid. I knew; I saw it in their eyes.

From that point on, things were different. Slowly, I drifted. I opened myself up to different kinds of people and realized that I had more in common with those who weren't part of the "popular group." I became more involved with my own interests. I became more self-assured. I found myself again. I found the best friend I had forgotten was inside of me, and she gave me the courage to run with my individuality. I wrote poetry and shared it. I hosted the TV news show at school, and I participated in other school events. I was respected, not by a few, but by everyone. I stood up for the little girl who was pushed around, for she was part of who I was now.

The faces reappeared, and I felt myself smile. I was at Homecoming. I made it. I looked out into the audience, and for once I felt understood. I had friends who cared about me, friends of the past and friends of the present. Friendships that had drifted in and out and in again. But most important, I had myself, and in her honor I wore that crown.

Rebecca Woolf

Realize You Are Responsible for Your Own Happiness

Nothing good ever comes from blaming others.
You can only change yourself.

A. B. Witt

Realize You Are Responsible for Your Own Happiness

Nothing can bring you peace but yourself.
Ralph Waldo Emerson

Sometimes we carry a sense of entitlement that makes us believe that other people owe us, that they are somehow responsible for our happiness. If we are sad, they need to give us their support. If we are lonely, they should keep us company. If we are in a relationship, our mates are supposed to protect us from pain. They should be sorry when we are mad and attentive when we are sad. They should promise that no matter what happens, they would never hurt us. These are impossible expectations.

Although it is normal and self-respecting to want others to treat you well, in the end it is your responsibility to take care of yourself. If you are in a situation in which you aren't being treated with respect, it is up to you to remove yourself from that situation.

You may have had a friend who constantly complains about the way her boyfriend treats her. The first time, you feel awful for her. The second time, you hold her hand and agree that the guy is a jerk. But after listening to her complaints again and again, the question inevitably becomes, "How much of this are you going to take before you stand up for yourself?" There is a fine line between being taken advantage of and *letting* yourself be taken advantage of.

You have to be honest with yourself about your circumstances. You have to face things that you might rather ignore. For instance, you may have a friend who turns out to be selfish and deceitful. Sadly, it becomes your responsibility to end the friendship if your attempts at working things out are unsuccessful.

Unrealistic expectations always end up hurting you. The more you believe others owe you, the sadder you are when they don't deliver. The "If he loved me, he would do this and he wouldn't do that" game is a setup for heartache. If you are able to say to yourself, "It is my job to be happy. It is my job to take care of myself, to be healthy, and to give myself the things I need," then you are owning your power to be happy or not.

You can't make rules in relationships to ensure that you never get hurt. You can't leave it up to someone else to make sure that you are happy. If you do, you will end up feeling disappointed and sometimes even brokenhearted. But you *can* take responsibility for your own happiness. You can be sure that you don't always end up in the position of the victim. You do this by acknowledging whose job it is to take care of you — yours. You do this by putting yourself in situations that are healthy, with people who are good to you and who understand friendship and commitment. When you find yourself unhappy, you look at your circumstances and figure out what you can do to change them. This is what it means to take responsibility for your happiness, and this is one way you can begin showing yourself the love you deserve.

A Girl's Guide to Being Beautiful

There is one moment in each day when you are completely in control of your own destiny. It is the moment you first open your eyes in the morning, the instant the first thought of the day skitters through your brain. That very first thought sets the mood for the rest of the day. In the wee hours of the morning, you can decide whether to embrace life as an ally or to declare war on the world.

If you give in to your inner demons and choose the latter, you can bid being beautiful farewell. *Nobody* looks good in a war. Beauty goes hand in hand with happiness, love, and peace. Even if you are not completely happy with your physical appearance, if you can possess those last three traits, you *will* be beautiful.

Kayla Knopp

It's Really Something

For years I was closed deep within, criticizing and constantly cursing my body and weight. Every calorie was an obsession, every fat gram an episode of unrelenting grief and hatred. It was all directed toward me, from me. I was my own worst villain. My entire day revolved around three meals. I'd spend as much time as I could panting on the StairMaster, swearing silently that no matter how much time or energy I put into the workout, it would never be enough.

I spent an entire summer in preparation for my thirteenth birthday. I dieted and denied myself so I could have a slice of cake at my party without remorse. I remember breaking this vow. We were at a family friend's house for a cookout. In a brief moment of weakness, I afforded myself a brownie and hated myself for it. I cried myself to sleep that night. The betrayal of self, of breaking a sacred personal vow, is the worst feeling there is. You begin to wonder who it is you can possibly trust if you can't even rely on yourself. Small wonder, then, that this memory has so faithfully remained imprinted in my mind.

I never had a mental image of my ideal body size or weight. I couldn't visualize myself in a finished state of perfection. The slim models in *Seventeen* weren't viable goals. To me, they were overweight. Once, when my cousin told me I had the body of a model, I panicked. I was *that size*? Was I so *fat*? How could it be that all of my toiling and dedication had no effect whatsoever on my body? Needless to say, intended comments of concern such as, "Oh my God, Katie, you're sooo skinny" or, "Ewww . . . I can count your ribs" made me beam with pride. At those times I truly felt I was closer to the final product that I was so blindly struggling toward.

I was well aware of the risk I was taking. Over and over people told me I wasn't healthy, that this thing called anorexia was fatal. But that didn't scare me. I knew why I got sick so easily — my immune system was down. I knew why my stomach and chest were being covered with a light peach fuzz and I was constantly cold — my body was trying to make up for the loss of fat. I knew why I had stopped menstruating — I simply didn't have enough resources in my system.

I researched anorexia thoroughly. Gradually I came to know the bitter tales, sometimes ending in death, of countless others with the same struggle. Of course these facts scared me — but not nearly as much as the idea of being "fat." I'd have rather died than gain weight. So the threat of death never even fazed me.

It got to the point where hunger was the norm. You know those awful hunger pangs you get in your stomach after a long day of hiking, swimming, or walking around? That's how it was for me. Constantly. And no matter how much I wanted them to go away, I couldn't reconcile this with the fact that I absolutely *had* to lose weight.

My parents and younger brother were both extremely concerned. My brother often called me "concentration camp girl," yelling at me constantly to eat something and telling me how disgusting I looked. I paid no attention. He was just a boy. He didn't understand these things. My parents, too, did everything they possibly could to get me to eat. There's a point for the family of someone with an eating disorder where all calm and tact vanish for the sole purpose of saving the life of a loved one. Family dinners became screaming matches — my father threatening to shove food down my throat if I wouldn't eat and me screaming back in tears that he was only trying to make me fat, to transform me into an unattractive, repulsively overweight object of derision. To me that was the sole motivation of both of my parents. Both my mother and father had always been large people. Again and again, I told myself I'd never end up like them. Their every attempt at trying to help me was, in my mind, a way to make me fat — just like they were. I rejected them both. I didn't want them to be near me, to touch me, or to show me any affection.

My mother was hit the hardest. All too often, I'd find her on her bed upstairs, quietly sobbing. It hurt me deeply. I wanted to make everything right, but I just didn't know how. I certainly didn't want to change what I was doing, especially when it had become such a significant part of who I was. My parents could have helped, but I kept pushing them away. It's strange how during the worst periods of your life, the first people you push away are the ones you need the most.

My life continued like this for nearly two years. I honestly don't know what happened to initiate my recovery. It seemed like a gradual culmination of events that slowly made their way into my subconscious and told me I needed to stop sometime soon. I needed to take my life seriously. One of these occurrences happened as I waited in line at the supermarket. Leafing through the magazines, I came upon a story about anorexia. The pictures detailed the struggle of a forty-year-old woman who at one point had weighed less than an average seven-year-old child. In the magazine were pictures of her at a "healthier" weight — she still looked terrifying. The pictures were horrific. I couldn't believe that this person, perfectly resembling a living skeleton, could have gotten so terribly thin. It scared me. I was actually disgusted — which is not to say that I resolved immediately to make myself better — but that image remained burned into my memory.

Another time I climbed the stairs of my house to find my tiny five-year-old sister in front of the full-length mirror, turning at all angles and prodding her thighs and stomach. I froze on the spot. Here was a little person who from the day of her birth had idolized me, had mimicked my every move. Until then I hadn't realized how closely she'd been watching. After a few minutes, she made an exasperated expression and declared, "I'm so fat." It was thoroughly disturbing to see my words and actions imitated so precisely. I knew that someday she could very easily take them seriously. Here, more than before, I realized that my actions had consequences beyond my own sphere of concern. That if not for anything else, I would have to recover for others. There were too many who loved me. I couldn't throw that all away.

Yet for all these influences, the ultimate driving force in my recovery was pure exhaustion. I was simply tired. I was tired of the relentless hunger. I was tired of the tears, the fighting, the constant arguments with my best friend who tried to make me realize that I wasn't fat by any definition, that I was dangerously thin. The taunts of my brother. The sleepless nights. I was worn out. I simply couldn't handle it anymore.

My recovery wasn't markedly abrupt or obvious. I gradually stopped looking on the nutrition label before eating things. I stopped weighing myself. And slowly — *very* slowly — but surely, I began to eat again.

Today you'd never guess that I once had barely hung on to my life. You'd never guess that I had anorexia. Very few of my friends know. Some of my extended family haven't a clue. I often forget about it myself, as it seems so long ago, and that girl is such a different person than the one I am today. Yet sometimes the realization that I pulled myself out of such an ordeal takes me by surprise, and I get a warm feeling all over when I think of it. I'm damn proud of having survived, of having overcome. Of having found that I *do* have worth, that I *can* endure, and that my problem wasn't insurmountable when all is said and done. I survived not only anorexia but also the plight of myself. It's really something.

Katie St. Martin

Don't Worry About What Others Think

Always be a first-rate version of yourself,
instead of a second-rate version of somebody else.

Judy Garland

Don't Worry About What Others Think

Spending your time worrying about what others think of you is certainly not uncommon. Everyone does it. But here are some things to keep in mind:

1. It is impossible to know what another person is thinking.
2. What other people think of you changes from moment to moment. Say, for instance, a friend tells you that someone said something bad about you. Of course, you feel hurt and you begin wondering all kinds of things: *What did I do to make this other person angry? Why is she saying these things? What can I do to get back at her?* But it is important to remember that this person could have been in a bad mood when she said what she did. Or she could have been trying to impress someone else. Or it is possible that something you did unintentionally hurt her feelings, and she is just reacting to that. We never really know what another person *thinks* simply by being told something he or she *said*.
3. You can't control what another person thinks about you. It might be really important to you that a particular person thinks highly of you. You might even try extra hard to get him or her to like you. But in the end, people are going to

think what they think, and it is usually something you can't do anything about.

4. When you are truly feeling good about yourself, you worry much less about what others think of you. This is the most important thing to remember.

Your time is much better spent working on what you think about yourself rather than trying to shape someone else's impression of you. This is the only thing that you have any control over, and it is the only thing that really matters.

A Definitive Choice

Did you know that corduroy pants come in dozens of colors? Throughout elementary school, I owned every one of them — red, yellow, brown, blue. Styles and fashion constantly change. When I was a kid, it just so happened that corduroy pants were about as out-of-style as you could get. And I was lucky enough to own them in every color made. In fact, I wore corduroy pants most every day.

When I walked, they would make a distinctive noise as the corduroy rubbed together: *swish, swish, swish, swish*. They made a frenzied *swishswishswish* when I attempted to play dodge ball in gym, and a small, uncomfortable *swwiiisssshh* as I nervously shifted in my seat while taking tests. My schoolmates called my pants an alert system. They would grin when they heard me coming and snicker as they watched me leave.

My wardrobe was a subject of great entertainment to them, a never-ending opportunity to make fun. Yet even if I had been dressed head to toe in designer clothing, I would not have been safe from their gossip and teasing — they were still armed with plenty of ammunition.

Truth be told, I was a very goofy-looking kid. I had an overbite, which made my already large front teeth appear even more prominent. I was taller than most kids my age, with gangly arms and legs, and I had my hair cut in a short, feathered style only to later find out that it consistently looked as though I styled it in a windstorm.

Matters worsened as I entered middle school. New braces (complete with rubber bands and headgear) were followed by the discovery that I was farsighted and needed to wear glasses for most of my schoolwork. My complexion began to rebel, my limbs were still too long for my body, and my hair, though longer, now suffered through a series of very bad perms.

As a result of my physical appearance, I was subjected to all of the embarrassment and ridicule childhood had to offer. I was called names, tripped in the hallways, and excluded from activities. I went out of my way to avoid the fortunate twelve- and thirteen-year-olds who already seemed to have adjusted to the physical changes of their bodies and the shifting social climate of early adolescence. Their confidence only made me feel more unattractive and unhappy. Each day, I walked into school with a knot in my stomach, counting the seconds until the bell rang.

My parents constantly reassured me that my painful situation would improve with time, and they were right. By the first year of high school, the braces came off, the contacts went in, and the hair calmed down into a plain, simple style. Those who had formerly teased me found new targets, and I was able to walk through the cafeteria without fear of embarrassment.

But much damage had been done. Convinced that I never wanted to be seen as an outcast again, I obsessed every morning over what to wear, attempting to look just like everyone else. I ate meticulously to maintain the super-skinny look which had become so popular and shopped only at the accepted trendy stores. Was I less goofy-looking? Perhaps. But did that mean I was happy with the way I looked? Not a chance. I constantly held myself up to others, comparing myself to what I considered perfect standards, and was never happy with what I saw. I sacrificed all of my own tastes and preferences, and in the process lost all sense of my own individuality.

During my first day of classes at college, I was hit with a reality that would change everything. Settling into my first class, I looked all around me and saw an amazing collection of different kinds of people. They were dressed in different ways and came from many different places. It occurred to me that we were each there to learn and to prepare for our future — not to compete for social status and not to struggle for acceptance. I felt as though a blindfold had been untied from my eyes, and I saw that maintaining a certain image and hiding my own personality here was not only unnecessary but also an injustice to myself.

I went home and tossed out every fashion magazine I had, realizing that articles that suggested I act or look a certain way, that told me how to "catch guys" or win friends, could never really help me discover who I was, what I wanted, or how to find happiness.

I suddenly understood that although people are often judged on their looks, labeled as one thing or another, and placed into categories, they have a choice in whether or not they allow themselves to be defined by others. All through school, I had accepted my label and my category as the truth. I now recognized that no one had the power to define who I was but *me* — and there was much more to who I was besides my physical appearance.

So I began to eat what tasted good, things that didn't say "low fat" on the package. I started to shop all over town, turning my boring wardrobe into a kaleidoscope of color and styles. These days, I choose to act and look like *myself* and never bother to wonder what others are thinking as they look me up and down. Do I look goofy? Sometimes. But am I happy? You bet. And every now and then I pull on a pair of corduroys . . . just for old time's sake.

Kelly Garnett

The Perfect Guy?

I met Kyle the summer before we started our junior year in high school. He was unlike any other guy that I had ever dated. Kyle was different. For some reason, I was drawn to his crooked grin and his dancing, light blue eyes. I loved the feel of my fingers running through his unruly auburn hair, and I loved it when he closed his arms around me and pulled me close. Not only was he different on the outside, but also on the inside. Kyle was the most caring, thoughtful, and wonderful guy that I had ever met. He never ceased to make me laugh, and he always listened to my trivial problems and would offer me a shoulder to cry on if I needed one. I thought I was the luckiest girl in the whole world. That is, until fall rolled around.

My friends were all dating the school hunks. You know the type: blond hair and a varsity letter or two. Or three. I felt inferior to my friends, and I was beginning to feel more and more ashamed of my relationship with Kyle.

One day, I was walking down the hall with a new friend, Angela, when those familiar arms enclosed my waist and I smelled the familiar scent of his cologne. Instead of feeling the flutter, the pride and happiness I had felt all summer, a shiver of nervousness and embarrassment traveled through me. I quickly pulled away.

"I've got to go," I told Kyle and practically ran down the hallway, dragging Angela with me. We stopped to catch our breath at the end of the hall.

"Why do you go out with him, anyway?" Angela looked disgusted. "I mean, do you ever take a look at what he wears? And it's, like, get a haircut! If I were you, I'd be mortified to even be seen with him! I swear, Katie, you can do so much better . . ."

As Angela babbled on about all of Kyle's faults I began to think, *Wow, maybe she's right. Maybe they're all right.* My friends had been trying to persuade me to break up with Kyle ever since school began. The more I thought about it, the more I was convinced that Kyle was nothing but an embarrassing accessory that had gone way out of style. I had made my decision.

When I got home, I picked up the phone and dialed Kyle's number. "Hi, Mrs. Lawlor? This is Katie . . . yeah, I'm fine . . . yeah, she's great, too . . . uh-huh . . . um, is Kyle there? Thanks." I nervously licked off my strawberry lip gloss as I listened to Mrs. Lawlor call her son.

Kyle got on the phone. "Katie, hi!" he exclaimed. "I haven't talked to you all day. You'll never guess what happened in Physics Club today . . ."

"No, wait, Kyle. I have to tell you . . . well . . ." I took a deep breath and spit it out. "I don't think that it's a good idea for us to be a couple anymore. It's just not working out. Kyle, it was fun, but it's over."

Silence.

"Kyle? I hope you're okay with this, because I mean, I . . ."

"No, I'm not okay. I love you, Katie, and I don't know what happened. Was it something I did or said?"

I couldn't talk anymore. I felt awful. He ended the call by saying he hoped I was happy. *Click.*

I placed the receiver back in the cradle, numbly walked over to my quote-a-day calendar, and habitually flipped to that day's page. I read the quote once, then twice, then again. What was written on it struck a chord in my soul.

Love is a little blind. When we love someone dearly,
we unconsciously overlook many thoughts.
Beatrice Saunders

Suddenly, I saw my life in a totally different light. Tears poured from my eyes. I buried my head in my pillow and didn't try to stop crying. I deserved the pain I was feeling. He was right. I was a terrible person. Guilt pricked at me like a thorn. All those times I had brushed him off in embarrassment . . . why? *Why?* Because he wasn't blond and built? Because he didn't have a flashy car or play a varsity sport? The stupidity of it all became so clear to me. Why hadn't I seen it before? I was wrong, and I knew what I had to do.

The next morning at school, I walked up to Kyle's locker. He looked at me and said nothing. I took a shaky breath and began: "Kyle, I am so sorry. I was wrong in breaking up with you. I cared too much about what other people thought and I was afraid they thought you were . . . well . . . weak and a nerd. I'm shallow and superficial and dumb, and if you never want to look at me again I wouldn't blame you. But please, can I please just maybe have . . ."

"Another chance?" he asked.

I nodded. Kyle cupped my chin in his hand. "Katie, I guess I knew that this was going on ever since we started school. I have always been afraid that I would lose you. I guess I'll forgive you, though, because after all I am weak, and any nerd would be lucky to have a girl like you."

I threw my arms around his neck, and I felt warmth and pride come over me.

My boyfriend Kyle. You know, he's unlike other guys. He possesses one of the greatest qualities any person could have: He is forgiving.

Katie Brennan

Circus Pants

My mother is big. Overweight. I don't like the word "obese." It sounds too much like "beast," which just doesn't fit my mother. I can remember my dad making comments about my mom's weight, sometimes behind her back and sometimes to her face. She would always use "I just had a baby" as a quick defense. "Just" at one point meant eight years ago.

I love my mom and dad very much, but when I was younger I guess you could say I was more of a "daddy's girl." My father is an excellent cartoonist and he has drawn many pictures of my mom over the years. She had these turquoise stretch pants with a small flower print that she wore an awful lot. My dad dubbed them the "circus pants," adding that somewhere there was a circus fat lady looking for her pants. A cartoon my dad drew, a "funny" that stands out in my mind, is one of my mom wearing the pants and sitting asleep in a rocking chair with my baby sister propped up on her stomach. Surrounding the chair were bags of popcorn and potato chips and a bottle of diet soda. My dad laughed about his little "work of art." I remember I laughed, too.

More vividly in my mind is the way my dad would stare intently at old photographs of my mom, petite and slender, taken when they were dating or first married. That was over twenty

59

years ago. I remember one time he set down a framed photograph of her in those days while shaking his head as if he were giving up hope or surrendering. Out loud he mused, "Do you think I would have married her if she looked the way she does now?" Looking up from the Barbie dolls I was playing with, I answered dumbly, not knowing if he was speaking to me or to himself, "No."

I felt a little embarrassed a few years later when my mom brought the circus pants to me when we were trying to assemble a clown costume for my fifth-grade Halloween parade at school. I kind of wanted to laugh, but I would have been too ashamed. She had long outgrown them, so I guess maybe they weren't as humorous anymore, but I ended up taking them anyway.

We had our Halloween party in Ms. Moslehi's class and then it was time to put on our costumes and parade around the school. I decided not to wear the pants, remembering how my dad and I had laughed at my mom as if she were a clown whenever she squeezed into them.

Without the circus pants, I decided that I'd wear the multicolored clown wig, a big red nose, and a polka-dot bow tie to march in the little parade. A girl in my class came up and asked me, "Where's the rest of your costume?" I told her that I didn't want to wear it because it was way too big for me, to which she responded, "Won't your mom be mad at you?" *I don't think so*, I thought to myself, *I don't think so*.

I am not ashamed of my mom. I probably was once. I think most of us are at some point in our young lives. I am not trying to bad-mouth my dad for his sometimes rude comments about my mom. My dad doesn't like the way he looks, either. He still goes on about how fat he is, and I can recall more than once his bragging about not eating for two or three days straight.

His "diet" may have rubbed off on his little girl, because I was going through some difficult times dealing with my appearance when I was in junior high. I had inherited my father's nose and my mother's bad eyesight. I had to wear clunky glasses to correct my vision. I had gone from a cute little girl to a scrawny, awkward adolescent with a flawed complexion and stringy red hair. I was learning how dad's criticism felt by that time as he told my mom one evening, "Put some makeup on your daughter." However, my self-criticism was far worse than anything other people could throw at me. After hearing all those angry voices in my head telling me that I was worthless, I stopped eating.

The other day I had a strange thought. The food I didn't eat, my mother probably ended up eating. That's how we dealt with pain. I starved it and she fed it. It was almost as though we were helping each other out in a way.

My decision to starve myself never got to the point where I needed professional help. It didn't last too long. I am now seventeen and at a healthy, average weight for a girl my age and height.

I am still far from loving myself or even accepting my flaws, and as I sit in front of the mirror cursing my hard-to-tame hair, my long nose, small chin, and acne-covered face, I realize something. My mom has never once said, "I'm fat" or, "I hate myself." She has never looked into a mirror and cried for hours like I have. I've never heard her talk bad about anyone else, either. She has a kind heart and a sweet spirit.

My father and I have found other ways to bond, without making fun of my mother. He is the pastor at our church and also works at my school, so I am very blessed to get to spend so much time with both of my parents. My dad and I have shared several hobbies, such as doll collecting and, more recently, music. We have been singing at church and at a nursing home for a few years and, since we started, I have learned to play guitar and I have learned a lot about my dad.

My mom works as a nurse at our local hospital. I go out there with my health occupations class and we make beds, give baths, and do other things that nurses' assistants do. I've noticed that my mom has remarkably kept her cool after over twenty years working as a nurse at this hospital. The staff and patients obviously love her. Sometimes, I'll come out of a patient's room and look at my mom down the hall filling out a patient's chart and I just beam with pride. My mom is like an angel to these patients and she is an inspiration to me. Even in circus pants.

Erica Dawn Jensen

Give Yourself a Break

*I am always doing the best I can; if I could do better,
I surely would. And when I can, I surely will.*

Robyn Posin

Give Yourself a Break

We give ourselves such a hard time. We're much harder on ourselves than we are on others. When our friends make mistakes, big or small, we offer them comfort and support. But rarely do we show ourselves the same understanding.

It's easy to think your mistakes are bigger or dumber than anyone else's. When a friend tries to reassure you by saying he or she has made a similar mistake, you might automatically assume yours is worse.

When giving yourself a break, you don't want to abandon self-control or self-observation. It is always important to think about your actions and examine the way you treat others. You want to be mindful of how you perform your everyday tasks and responsibilities, and you certainly don't want to go around hurting people and not taking care of things for which you are responsible. However, self-observation is very different from self-judgment. Observation is objective and is necessary for learning; judgment is negative, and negativity *never* makes a difficult situation better. When you beat yourself up for something you have done, *no good comes from it.*

Giving yourself a break simply means not punishing yourself again and again for the same mistakes. When you obsess over something you did that you now regret, or when you hate yourself for a problem you have, you make it that much harder to heal and move on. When you choose to take action, as opposed to just feeling guilty, you'll see positive changes in your life.

It is also important to do things that help you relax and let go of the stresses that build up each day. Being a teen today means you are under a lot of pressure to achieve: get good grades, get into a good college, make and keep friends, and much more. Then there are all the things you are under pressure *not* to do. It is very important to make time in your day to relax and give yourself a break from whatever stresses you out.

When I asked teens what things they do to give themselves a break, the most common answers were: "listen to music," "talk to friends," and just simply "retreat to my bedroom." Whatever it is that helps you to relax, be sure to take time to do it every day. This is one very important way to begin being a friend to yourself.

My Worst Enemy

He used to look at me like I was the most beautiful girl in the entire universe. He often gazed at me, the corners of his eyes wrinkled by a sweet grin on his lips, and told me that I was an angel who had swooped down from heaven just for him. There were many moments in our relationship when I convinced myself that Brian and I were destined to spend our lives together just because when he looked at me with his adoring eyes I felt, for the first time ever, like I was beautiful.

When I was with Brian, I was at peace with myself. Unfortunately, things were not so tranquil when I was without him. My self-esteem was terribly low, and by the time I was seventeen, I was painfully aware that this was a serious problem. Instead of solving the problem, I opted to hide it and pretend like I was perfectly content with myself. I let Brian give me the love that I couldn't give myself. I didn't want him to know that my reflection was my own worst enemy. I didn't want him to know that I spent nights crying because my hips were too wide and my thighs were too fat. I didn't want him to know that the girl he loved didn't love herself.

"Emily, you're amazing," he would whisper softly, tickling my ear while my heart threatened to burst from happiness.

As the months wore on, my lack of self-confidence began to

67

show through. Brian would say, "Emily, why don't you wear that shirt?" And I would argue, "It makes my hips look too big." He would shrug, as boys often do when they can't quite understand the reasoning of the female mind, and the subject would be dropped. The problem was, moments like that began to show up more and more often in our relationship, and Brian started to get frustrated.

"Emily, you're beautiful! Why do you have to get so jealous? You know I love you!" And even though I knew this, every time I saw Brian talking to other girls, my mind instantly feared he had finally realized that I really wasn't as gorgeous as he had thought.

"I can't deal with this anymore," he announced one day. "How can you love me if you can't even love yourself? I love you for you. But you have to find out what it is that makes you so scared of who you really are. You have to stop being so negative about yourself." He left after that and I was stuck, all alone, with my own worst enemy.

In time, I realized my relationship with myself was just like a relationship I have with anyone else. In order to make it better, it was necessary to nurture it. Just like I spend time with the people I love, I had to spend time with myself. I had to learn and grow and hold my own hand instead of slapping it away.

Of course, it took me many painful months to discover this truth. I took the breakup with Brian really hard and verbally bashed myself time and time again. Ironically, I was punishing myself for not loving myself. I actually believed that I was a plague to society who didn't deserve to live on the same planet with loving, accepting people like Brian. When I looked in the mirror, I absolutely despised the person with the puffy, red eyes and unwashed hair who stared back at me.

Developing self-acceptance was a process that occurred slowly, but gradually I began to smile at my reflection. Little things like a guy in chemistry class calling me cute, shopping for clothes that were more fitting and flattering, and discovering new interests and talents contributed to the foundation for my whole new perspective on me. Giving myself a hard time hurt me. Accepting and loving myself nurtured me. I began to feel more energetic and I was excited about even the smallest things. It's incredible how my worst enemy turned out to be my best friend once I made some humble yet necessary changes. I can honestly say I like myself now. And I've got a feeling things are just going to keep getting better.

Emily Starr

Start Being

My mind a chaotic cacophony of thoughts.
I walk barefoot through the cool grass
yearning to delight only in the feeling
of the crisp blades between my toes —
To forget for once the heaviness in my stomach
and the positioning of my clothes.
I want to be able to not have to think
about how I shouldn't be thinking so much.
To delight in the warmth of the sun on my skin
and the company of thick laughter.
I need to let it drown out the
doubting of my own self-worth
and the need to be reassured of my place here.
I need to stop thinking so much
and start being.

Kathryn Litzenberger

Sweeten Your Self-Talk

A Native American elder once described his own inner struggles in this manner: "Inside of me there are two dogs. One of the dogs is mean and evil. The other dog is good. The mean dog fights the good dog all the time." When asked which dog wins, he reflected for a moment and replied, "The one I feed the most."

George Bernard Shaw

Sweeten Your Self-Talk

I'm such a loser. I can't believe I said that. I look so fat in these pants. He would never go out with someone like me. Why can't I look like her? I can't do anything right. Everyone else has it so much easier than I do. What is wrong with me, anyway?

Does any of this sound familiar to you? If you were to actually write down every negative thing you say to yourself in a day, you would be shocked. Have you ever wondered why you say such cruel things to yourself?

A lot of it comes from habit. Your mind repeats the negative things that may have been said to you by teachers, parents, or siblings. For instance, I grew up with three older brothers. We used to say some pretty mean stuff to one another. One of their favorite mean things to say to me was, "Nobody likes you." They certainly never intended to program a negative self-image into the mind of their beloved sister — this is just one of the things siblings do. But things people say to you can become part of your thinking, without you even realizing it. This is why it is so important to begin paying attention to your thoughts and becoming aware of the way you speak to yourself.

Thoughts you have about yourself are called self-talk. Positive thoughts about yourself are called positive self-talk. Negative thoughts about yourself are called negative self-talk.

Get into the habit of practicing positive self-talk whenever you have a few minutes alone. Remind yourself of compliments you have received in the past. Then think about what *you* like about you. What compliment would you give yourself? When you say nice things to yourself, it has the same effect as when others say kind things to you. Your feelings about yourself become more positive, you feel happier, and your self-confidence is boosted.

When you are lying in bed at night, get into the habit of going over your day and remembering the things you did that you feel good about. What did you do that you are proud of? Think about the small things — they count a lot. Every time your mind wanders to something negative, try to bring your focus back to the positive. At first you may find this difficult, but as you keep doing it, it gets easier.

You may worry that thinking positive thoughts about yourself will make you conceited. That won't happen. There's a big difference between thinking you're a good person and thinking you're the best person around. And even though this should never be the motivating factor, it doesn't hurt to consider who other people will be more attracted to: someone who is confident and secure, or someone who is constantly thinking about how stupid she is.

Thinking bad thoughts about yourself will make you feel bad. Thinking good thoughts about yourself will make you feel good. It's that simple. Sweetening your self-talk takes time. But as you practice saying kind things to yourself, your self-acceptance will grow.

Through the Eyes of a Stranger

It is often said that seeing is believing; yet when it comes to one's own reflection, I've never found that statement to possess any truth. In fact, hearing is often believing. There was once this girl, and every day when she saw me she would sneer and say, "You're hideous." "You're fat." "Your complexion is horrible." "Your outfit looks stupid." She said these things over and over again till I just buried my head in my hands and sobbed uncontrollably every time I saw my own reflection. *She was right*, I told myself. She was right about everything. The words were constantly echoing in my mind, ringing in my ears, screaming at my face. And that girl wasn't a bully at school or an enemy on the soccer field. She didn't have a crush on my boyfriend or any reason to hate me with so much passion. She was me. My tormentor was myself.

"You can't wear that." "You can't talk to him." "You can't get an A." It went beyond the mirror, so that even when I wasn't gazing at my reflection, the voice was still there. No aspect of my life went untouched. The word "can't" consumed my mind on a daily basis. The things I once could do, I no longer enjoyed. While playing basketball, for example, shots I once would've taken ended up being passes. I missed easy layups because I was constantly questioning my own abilities. I was afraid of making a mistake, afraid of having to deal with looking foolish in front of everyone.

It became second nature to pass instead of shoot, to avoid mirrors, to feel like every mistake I made somehow proved to myself that I was as horrible as that voice kept telling me I was. I wanted to be the best at everything, but I was so afraid of failure that I missed out on opportunities that would have opened so many new doors. Even when talking to people, I could hardly relax and enjoy the conversation because I was so afraid of saying something stupid, something clumsy, something uninteresting.

I went through most of high school frowning at my reflection, constantly afraid of failure, until one day when I went to see a play in a big theater house. I vividly remember walking up a flight of crimson-carpeted stairs and looking to my right where another girl was walking on another staircase. There was something familiar about her and I thought to myself, *Wow. She's really pretty.* When I reached the top, I looked over to have a better look at this stranger, but I found myself standing there alone, looking at my own reflection. It was confusing at first because I honestly didn't know I was looking at a mirror and that I had been the entire time, but something clicked in my brain right then. It was like a slap across the face. It was like waking up for the first time in years. There she was, this girl who I had thought — not knowing that I was looking at my own reflection — was beautiful. I was so used to hating what I saw in the mirror that I couldn't even see anything beyond my faults. I didn't even recognize myself!

Now, when I look at my reflection, I see myself. I see all of the good things; I see all of the unique features that make me original. The voices in my head are soft and forgiving. I don't use the word "can't" anymore. I got lucky because I saw myself through a stranger's eyes. If only everyone could see how they truly look and not how they think they look, so many problems people battle with could be extinguished. Next time you gaze at your reflection, smile. It's surprising how completely different that person staring back at you will look.

Emily Starr

My Daily Self-Evaluation

I stare in the mirror,
Pinching the skin around my stomach,
Molding it into the ideal shape.

I wish that I could look like her,
The girl in the magazine.
I compare our hair and teeth,
Our skin and our lips.

With every look my self-esteem vanishes.
Losing confidence, my smile soon fades.
My flaws seem endless and numbered
As I quickly fall into a state of sadness,
And put on a baggy sweatshirt,
Concealing my imperfect figure,
Letting go of my dreams and pretending I don't care.

Slowly and realistically I begin to accept
My image and identity, repeating to myself
That I am the only me, and that is a good thing.

Jenny Sharaf

Let Others Love You

To love and be loved is to feel the sun from both sides.

David Viscott

Let Others Love You

How many times have you sat around thinking that you wish someone loved you, or you wish your phone would ring, or you wish you had more friends, or you wish you didn't feel so lonely? Everyone has days when their feelings of loneliness are overwhelming, and for some reason those are usually the days that the phone doesn't ring.

However, if you are like most of us, there are just as many times when love is coming toward you and you push it away. Either you are invited out by friends but you're not in the mood to go, or the nice things people say to you just make you feel uncomfortable. Someone tells you how pretty you look or that you did a good job, and you turn it around and respond, "Me? I look awful today!" or, "What? I did a terrible job." Sometimes it seems hard to let others love you.

I have a friend who is often sad because she feels that her boyfriend doesn't say nice things to her like, "I love you," or "You look really pretty tonight." I can understand how she feels — everyone likes to hear nice things. One night I was going somewhere with my friend and her boyfriend and I heard him tell her she looked really good. He said, "I love those pants. Are they new?" Her response surprised me. She was angry. "No, they're not," she snapped. "You've seen these pants before. I've worn them, like, ten times in the last month." She hadn't even heard his compliment. I was really confused. What was she angry about? Later she told me that he doesn't usually pay attention to what she is wearing, and she found it insulting that he had never noticed those pants before. She felt he was just handing her a line, or maybe he was trying to look good in front of me. Huh? I told her I thought she should accept the compliment and let herself feel good about it and thank him. Put simply, I suggested she let herself feel loved.

Love doesn't always come dressed in the package we want. It doesn't arrive on our schedule and it doesn't follow our guidelines and rules. It is love. It is intangible, unpredictable, and certainly uncontrollable. This is what can make it painful, but this is also what makes it so wonderful. We need to remember to be grateful and honored by its presence in our lives.

Be careful not to make rules where love is concerned. Be careful to not let it pass you by just because it doesn't present itself the way you think it should.

When a friend or loved one offers support or pays you a compliment, allow yourself to be receptive. When you are hurting and in need of nurturing, let others love you. When you feel uncomfortable being on the receiving side of love, try to remember: The more love you are able to receive, the more love you will have to give — to others and to yourself. Open your heart and let it in.

What One Teen Thinks

I am sitting at my kitchen table with five close friends gathered around me at a summer slumber party. Half-filled pizza boxes, ice cream cartons, and soda bottles are strewn around us. We are breathless and flushed from a pillow fight over a competitive game of cards. *NSYNC blasts from my radio. Ahhh . . . a classic teenage girl get-together.

Maybe a little *too* classic. As can be expected whenever a group of teenage girls get together, the topic of conversation inevitably turns to weight.

"I am so fat!" one of my pencil-thin friends says.

And, of course, a chorus of "No, no! You're *thin. I'm* the one who's fat!" fills the air.

And soon it turns into the usual argument about who needs to lose the most weight. As if they *want* to be considered overweight! I'm the only one who doesn't join in the argument. I bite into my greasy pizza slice deliberately and roll my eyes as a ninety-pound fifteen-year-old declares she needs to go on a diet.

"What are you talking about?! You're anorexic enough already!" I blurt out.

And she takes this as a compliment. She tries to act offended, as is socially acceptable, but really her mouth is already turning up in the beginnings of a smile and her face glows despite herself. Sickened, I fill my bowl with chocolate ice cream.

"Well, what about you?" she finally retorts. "*You're* thin."

And it's true. I am thin. But not anorexic thin, and not because I starve myself.

I'm 5'11" and seem to have an extremely high metabolism; I'm just built to be slender. Overall, I'm happy with my weight, but just living in this society, it's an everyday struggle not to become anorexic. There are days when I accidentally miss a meal and think, *Well, maybe it's for the best.* I don't usually exercise for athletic reasons. And I absolutely hate the way I always have to get size large clothes in department stores because everything else looks like it's made for super-skinny little pixies.

But even now, it's better than it used to be. There was a time when I really did believe I was fat.

I was about twelve. It started because I noticed most teenage girls criticizing their bodies, especially their weight. Therefore, I felt that in order to truly become a teenager, I should be unhappy with my appearance as well. After a while, I really began to believe I was fat. I began to weigh myself regularly on the scale in my parents' bathroom.

When my sister found out, she was furious. One day, on my ritual trip to the bathroom, she ran in ahead of me and locked the door. When I realized she would not let me in to weigh myself, I grew more and more upset. I banged on the door for almost an hour. Finally, I went back to my room and cried, completely defeated.

My sister came and hugged me. Her eyes were full of concern and I could hardly look into them. I was full of shame because I had cared so much about what I weighed. And yet I was angry because I didn't know what number the scale would have read back to me that day.

My sister told me, "Bonnie, you're beautiful no matter what you weigh. Your weight doesn't matter." But it would be years before I would believe it.

For a long time afterward, I still looked at the scale in my parents' bathroom longingly, and sometimes waited for my sister to leave the house before going in there. Gradually, the scale became less and less important to me. After a while, I no longer even cared. The only time I would find out my weight was at the doctor's office. My friends are surprised that I don't know my own weight, but I have grown very proud of that fact. I am finally happy with the way I look.

Bonnie Kellman

Dying to Be Thin

You fat cow. You'll never be anything with your stomach protruding out the way it does. You are a whale. These are the thoughts that ran through my head every single day for years while I would stand in front of the mirror.

I fought the disease for over five years. It began in the middle of seventh grade. I was chubby — and angry at the world. My parents had decided to move to a new town, and I didn't want to leave my friends and the town I had grown up in. I started restricting my food intake while at school by not eating lunch, but skipping meals at home was more difficult. I didn't lose much weight, and eventually I went back to my normal eating habits.

I made friends at my new school, but it wasn't easy. I started flirting with danger again: restricting my eating and lying to my parents about it. I'd tell them I had eaten when I hadn't eaten at all. Friends got concerned and alerted the health teacher. She tried talking to me, but I would deny everything. I ignored my mother, who noticed that I was losing weight. This pattern continued for a couple of years.

During my sophomore year, things began to spin out of control. Friends were more concerned than ever, so I went to talk to my English teacher, whom I trusted. Palmer, as I call her, let me

86

have lunch in her room since eating around a lot of people was difficult for me. She'd force me to drink Gatorade to help my electrolytes. She supported me, but she wasn't quite sure how she should deal with the situation. Eventually, after nearly passing out during a choir trip, I agreed to tell my parents what was going on. It wasn't easy, but I managed. My mother got on the phone with a psychologist right away.

I was referred to a nutritionist, Donna, who gave me a meal plan that I tried to follow. Donna would weigh me every week. Then my grandfather died and I was very upset. I didn't want to think about anything but how fat I was. So I stopped eating again.

One morning, after walking up the stairs to Palmer's class, I collapsed. My friend Jen was there to help me up and get me to class. I kept telling her I was fine and put my head down on my desk. She knew me too well, though, and alerted Palmer, who alerted the school nurse, who alerted my parents. My mom and dad drove me to three different hospitals that day. I wasn't admitted to an eating disorder unit because our insurance wouldn't cover it. But the experience scared me into eating again.

I started "dieting" again at the start of my senior year. I felt huge and wanted to be skinny. I hated myself. My cousin, our friends, and I drove to North Carolina one weekend. I wasn't eating much and I wasn't very strong. On our way home we stopped to sleep at my aunt's house in Virginia. I was so out of it that I had to be carried into the house. My aunt Joni is a nurse. I had to fight with her not to go to the hospital. She wanted me to eat something, but I was terrified of food.

My dad drove me to Community Medical Center early one

morning in October. I had an ear infection and I was really weak. Dad told the nurse I wasn't eating. Tests and blood work revealed that my kidney and liver were damaged, I was severely dehydrated, and my vital signs were off. I was taken to another hospital and admitted into the eating disorder unit, despite my protests.

I had an IV in me for days. Luke, the name I gave my IV pole, and I were stuck together way too long. The nurses had to keep switching where the needle went into my hand because it was so painful. Due to the liquids Luke fed me, I gained some weight. I wanted Luke out so badly, but the nurses, doctors, and nutritionists said my vital signs were still wacky. I thought I was too huge to be in a hospital among skinny girls.

A little over six weeks later, right before Thanksgiving, I was discharged. I immediately started restricting my food intake, but eventually, with the help of my nutritionist, I slowly started eating again. Going back to school was strange, but Palmer let me spend my lunch hour with her, and that made things easier.

In all, I missed 104 days of school my senior year, but still managed to graduate. I pretty much have my eating disorder under control these days. I still have occasional bad days, but I am at a healthy weight now. Life isn't easy, and sometimes it's hard not to slip back into the throes of anorexia. I was lucky; I survived. I had people who cared about me, and for that I will be forever grateful. I know I'm not perfect, and I also know that nobody else is either — and I find great comfort in that.

Danielle Guardino

A Love for Myself

With tears stinging my cheeks, I rush into the bathroom trying to throw up my aching heart. It feels broken and I want it out of me. As I lean over the porcelain bowl, I watch my tears drip into the water below me, and all at once my hurt and sadness turn to fear. Here I am again, throwing up my emotions because they're too much for me to handle.

I don't think that I was ever "fat" per se, but I definitely could have been thinner. I was a perfectly normal teenage girl living in Los Angeles, home of the beautiful. Looking around a world where the media-image ideal begins and having gone to school with celebrities' children, I was constantly reminded of my differences — "uniqueness," they told me. Walking down the streets of Hollywood with my oh-so-tiny friends, it seemed that there were only two sizes of people — the little breakable ones, and the obese. As I watched all of my size-zero friends raid each other's closets while folding my arms in an attempt to hide my stomach, I knew that I didn't fit their world. I decided I must be one of the obese.

Like everyone else, I tried dieting and exercising, and I did lose some weight. However, my attempts were usually short-lived. I couldn't seem to find the motivation to stick with it. I ate until I was sick, and one day I actually made a decision to become bulimic. I went to school the next day and casually threw up everything I ate. After all, that's what a bulimic person does, I figured.

When I threw up my food, I felt like I was correcting an emotional distortion that told me I was somehow inferior to others. When I was sad, or reprimanded by my parents, I would throw up the pain. Everything about me was too big. I felt like an ogre. I was an oversized monster with acne and stringy hair, although in reality the occasional zit that developed on my otherwise clear complexion was hardly acne and my hair was actually long, thick, and silky. I just didn't see it that way. As the bulimia developed into a daily habit, I still didn't see it as a problem. It became difficult to hold food down as my stomach became weaker. But what was a little nausea in the long run? I felt thinner when I threw up, even though I really wasn't, and as long as I *felt* thinner, I was okay.

As my problem worsened and my self-esteem plunged to dangerously low levels, I still had no desire to quit. Spiraling downward, I nearly missed the hand that was reaching out for me. Shaun was my first love. He was gorgeous and he thought the same about me. When someone else thinks you are beautiful, you start to believe it yourself. He was the first person I told about my problem. It made him sad to think that I would do anything so harmful to myself, and I began to feel guilty every time I hung my head over the toilet. When I threw up, I would promise myself that I was not going to tell Shaun about it. But I just couldn't lie to him and often ended up sobbing on his shoulder.

He started to teach me how to eat better and exercise more

effectively. I began to write about my feelings when I was up-set about something, and slowly my wall of self-pity and self-loathing began to crumble. I started to feel better about myself, and I had someone I truly trusted with whom I could share my emotions. Slowly, I began to conquer my bulimia. Shaun expressed his growing pride for me and lent the constantly needed encouragement not to give up. "One day at a time," he recited to me, a cliché I have never forgotten.

Then one day I stopped. It was almost as if I knew that I was never going to throw up again. I didn't need to. I felt good about myself and had found a more constructive emotional release in my writing.

Unfortunately, we were graduating soon, and Shaun's plan was to travel to Europe for a year. So we broke up. And there I was again, thrust over this bottomless, watery pit trying to throw up my aching heart. As I stared into the reflective water, all at once memories started rushing back at me, and I stopped crying. I stood up and walked out of the bathroom, leaving the water untainted. Overwhelmed by the fear of what I had almost done, I called Shaun and told him what had happened. He asked me if I was going to throw up once he left and I could honestly say, "No, I won't." And I didn't.

Shaun's gone now and I am always happy to receive the in-frequent, but oh-so-exciting letter about his travels. My heart aches for him, but I will move on. Although he is gone now, he left me with the best gift anyone has ever given me . . . a love for myself.

Rose Lannutti

Start Small

Do what you can, with what you have, where you are.

Theodore Roosevelt

Start Small

You have probably had the experience of setting goals for yourself that were too large and unrealistic. You haven't studied all semester so you give yourself two days to learn everything for the big test, or you decide to give up a bad habit you've had for years right *now*. You promise yourself that you will bring up your grades by getting all A's on everything for the rest of the term. Or you decide you are going to save all your money and not waste a cent on clothes or makeup. The problem is that the first time you slip, it's tempting to just give up completely. You set yourself up for failure when you set goals that are too big to realistically achieve. That is why starting small is so important. By setting goals that you can accomplish, you give yourself a better chance of reaching those goals and feeling good about yourself.

If you want to get healthy, start small. Ask your parents if you can talk to your doctor about good nutrition. If you want to feel more confident in a bathing suit, think of an exercise you enjoy and find time to do it more often. Whatever the challenge, start small enough to ensure your success. Each time you succeed, you will be motivated to keep moving in the right direction. Let yourself feel successful — you will be amazed at how motivating that can be.

It is very helpful to write your goals in a journal or notebook that you use only for this purpose. You can write about a big goal and then break it up into smaller pieces that are easily achievable for you. Or you may want to work on one or more smaller goals. As you succeed at the goals you have set for yourself, you can check them off and allow yourself to feel good about what you have accomplished. Celebrating your successes is very important.

Try not to get stuck in the "I've tried this before and it never worked, so why bother trying again?" mode. And don't get hung up feeling that the goal you are working on is too big and therefore impossible to achieve. It is easy to feel this way — we all have — but the trick is to not let your fear of failure stop you from doing whatever it is that you are trying to accomplish.

If you have a big problem, like drug addiction or an eating disorder, you may think, *This is too big. I can't turn it around now.* It is at these times that it is so important to have compassion for yourself. Remember, you didn't get where you are in one day and you won't make things entirely better in one day, either. But you *can* take that first step, which is always the most important one.

Army Tank vs. the Ethiopian

The roar of the cafeteria is deafening. I can't stand this school. I want to get up from this cluttered table, run out the blue double doors into the land of the free, and never come back. But I don't. I stay and watch everyone else eat. It reminds me of cows at a feeding trough. Chew, chew, chew, swallow. Faces contorted into digestive ecstasy. It repulses me. I do not eat. I haven't eaten lunch in years. I do not deserve to eat. I am fat, ugly, and stupid. I deserve to die.

At home I lie and say I've eaten a big lunch. I say that I only want salad for dinner. Some think I have an "eating problem." My parents, especially my father, make up jokes and nicknames about my weight. My father's favorite nickname for me is "Ethiopian."

I have one best friend in the world. That's all I need. Since I have lost so much weight, she can put me in my place with the tact of an army tank. My best friend puts my not eating and my diet talk together and names it: anorexia. I tell her I'm normal, knowing full well I'm not. I feel achy all over, bones protrude from my rear so much it hurts to sit, and I can't concentrate.

She learns about my diet pills and my feeble attempts at making myself throw up and notices my sensitivity to cold because I shiver all of the time even though I wear layers of clothes.

97

Her mother notices, too. So do a lot of people. They gape at my thinness.

My best friend's family makes me eat whenever I come over. It's annoying sometimes, but I know they watch me because they care. One night they take us out to Taco Bell. I fervently deny my hunger. I am forced to eat a taco anyway. I feel like a fat, disgusting pig. I run outside into the cold December air. I have to get rid of the food in my stomach. I go to the Dumpsters behind the restaurant and try to make myself vomit. I can't do it, so I walk back to the van. My best friend and her family are already waiting there, staring at me. My best friend automatically shifts into her army tank mode and gets me. She would keep it up, too, were it not for her parents. She keeps accusing me of puking. I deny it, but I can tell neither she nor her family believes me. It's true — I really didn't throw up, I only tried. The whole way home she keeps saying, "Did you enjoy your puke? I know you did. I know you puked. Did you enjoy it?" I want to hit her. I want to scream, kick, and cry like a two-year-old. I want to yell, "I'm sorry, I'm out of control, help me!" Instead, I keep my mouth shut.

I sleep on the couch at her house that night, enveloped by the heat from the kerosene heater in the doorway. I think about what I have done because of a stupid taco and realize that there have been a lot of "tacos" in my life. Before falling asleep, I decide to get help.

Five years of my life have been wasted. I can't get those years back. But I've kept my promise to myself to do better each day. I eat something every three hours so my stomach can get used to the feeling again. Sometimes the pain in my stomach is so in-

98

tense that I want to stop eating again, but I don't. It hurts emotionally, too, because I look at myself and still see fat. I don't know how much I weigh, nor do I want to know. I know that I have most likely gained weight, which is not a bad thing. I'm not perfectly well yet. I remind myself that all I can do is get a little bit better with each day. And each day getting better feels good.

Axton Betz

Prisoner of the Mind

Stone walls do not a prison make, nor iron bars a cage.
Richard Lovelace

Some are locked behind iron grates, others are prisoners of their own fears, which can be even harder to unlock. I became a prisoner of my mind.

I'm a fifteen-year-old girl with blond hair, blue eyes, and dyslexia. Dyslexia is as much a part of me as any other trait I've inherited from my mom and dad. Just the way my blond hair encourages some to make certain assumptions about my intelligence — Question: How do blond brain cells die? Answer: Alone (ha, ha, ha) — so does my dyslexia. In case you've never heard of dyslexia, I'll give you a brief explanation. It's a language-based learning disorder, which does not affect your intelligence, but makes reading and writing extremely challenging.

Needless to say, having dyslexia made me feel different from those around me. I was fine socially until the kids in my first grade class started learning to read. I loved books and wanted to unlock the mystery behind the secret code my friends had cracked so easily. Unfortunately, I was destined to stare blankly at a jumble of senseless words. My teachers sighed in frustration and made me read and reread the words on the page until I got them right. My halting and stuttering recitation caused the other kids to laugh and tease me. I hated them and the world around me for making me feel so strange.

My parents brought me to be evaluated by a psychologist who told them I was dyslexic. They hired a reading tutor to work with me at home, and through years of work my reading greatly improved. But the damage to my self-esteem was already done.

At school, I felt like a visitor to a foreign country who didn't speak the language. I grew more frightened with each passing day. I wanted out of this strange world, and the solution was simple — create my own. And so the performances began. Every day I'd concoct some ridiculous illness that made leaving home impossible. I don't think my mom really bought it, but she became exasperated from the fights. Once I got going, she knew there was no way she'd ever get me out the door. And so she'd sigh and shake her head, giving in to me once again.

My world became a safe haven of TV, the computer, food, and sleep. Best of all I loved television because everything on it seemed to result in a happy ending. I watched so much television that to this day I cannot tell you who our Secretary of State is, but I can recite every theme song from every TV show I've seen, which is pretty sad. The TV people became the friends I could turn to for comfort. Life is so much easier when you don't have to participate.

By middle school, staying home was a way of life for me. I knew just how many days I could get away with skipping without the school district complaining. It was a delicate balance. On the rare days I did show up for school, by mid-morning I was heading for the nurse's office. I can joke about it now, but back

101

then the school nurse was my warden and my best friend. I suppose she thought she was doing the right thing by releasing me when I was "sick," or maybe it was simply easier to give in.

Should somebody have noticed the warning signs — the school nurse, my parents, the teachers? Maybe, but nobody said anything to me except this one science teacher in middle school. When I did show up for his class, he would have the entire room stand up and applaud. It was a sarcastic and cheap attempt to get laughs at my expense. I'd smile along with the rest, but inside I was mortified. He did this every time I came to class . . . and so I began to show up less and less.

School and the outside world became smaller and smaller. It's funny how one fear can spread like a disease, infecting parts of your life you'd never expect. Even going to the mall became an anxiety-producing experience. Would I run into the kids from school? Would they laugh at me? Innocent things which had never frightened me before began to spook me — like escalators. I'd stand at the top of those quickly moving steps, peering down at their sharp metal teeth. What if I took a wrong step and hurtled to my death? I'd stand there balancing at the top step, deciding whether to get on, and then end up backing away to let people go ahead of me. Finally I'd turn away, deciding it was better not to take any chances.

The world I created eventually became a prison of its own. I'd watch TV shows where girls hung out together, laughed together, shared secrets and private moments. By the time I was a freshman in high school, it was not enough for me to live through the characters on TV. I wanted that to be *my* life. But I was so afraid. It was much easier to convince myself that tomorrow I'd make the step back into the world. But, tomorrow never seemed to come.

By now my absences at school had escalated to such a point that the district could no longer ignore them. They complained to my parents, who pleaded with me to go to school. I made false promises to them that I would make a serious attempt. They wanted to believe me, and I wanted to believe me.

One Friday night there happened to be a story on *20/20* about people who have a disorder known as agoraphobia. They were afraid to leave their own homes — just like me. According to the story, the world agoraphobics build for themselves eventually shrinks smaller and smaller. For some it even caves in on them. There was one poor guy who was living in his bathroom. It may sound ridiculous, but he really believed that if he left the safety of his tiled world, he might die. Was I destined for this end? I decided right then and there that I had to break free before my fears swallowed me whole. I could no longer wait for someone to rescue me.

The story on *20/20* described a process called desensitization, through which subjects are slowly introduced back into the world. I decided this was the way out for me as well. I began to force myself to go to school with more frequency. I took baby steps in trying new things, so as not to overwhelm myself. The world had changed a lot since I'd actively been in it. I had changed a lot, too. I started returning to the mall and even tackled those dreaded escalators. I found one that was not heavily trafficked. I stood nervously at the top with my right foot perched over the steps. I took a deep breath, synchronizing the movement of my foot along with the moving steps, and went for it. I actually rode the escalator. And then I did it again, and again. I did it about ten times in a row. The people watching probably thought I was crazy, but I wanted to make sure that I could do it until it didn't scare me anymore. And the more I did it, the less scary it became.

With the same aplomb, I took on making friends. At first it wasn't easy since my social skills were pretty rusty. But just as with each trip on the escalator, making friends and socializing became less and less frightening. I started out one-on-one or in small social groups, working my way up to an actual high school dance. I still sweat and shake at one of those things, but part of the reason is because I'm dancing!

In the end I've learned that sometimes we just have to face our fears, and that when we don't take leaps, we limit our chances for a real life. Also, the fears we concoct in our minds are far worse than any reality — to this day I have never hurtled to my death on any escalator steps (obviously, or I would not be here to tell my story). But it's these self-made fears that imprison us the most effectively and are the hardest to surmount. It was not the kids, or the teachers, or my parents, or even my dyslexia that was my jailer — it was really me. And in the end, I was the only one who could set me free.

Janice Deegan,
as told to C. S. Dweck

Do It for You

The person who seeks all their applause from outside has their happiness in another's keeping.

Claudius Claudianus

Do It for You

Don't do it for your parents. Don't do it for your boyfriend.
Don't do it for your best friend. Don't do it for your teachers.
Do it for you.

Many times you set out to make changes in your life because you think somebody else will like you more. You brush your hair and put on lipstick because you think the guy in second period will notice. Or you start going to the gym because all of your friends are losing weight and you want to fit in. Making a change in your life can be a good thing, but if you do it for other people — instead of for you — it will not have as much meaning. If you are thinking about changing your look, do it because you will feel better. Don't do it for your crush. If you want to start a new exercise program, do it so you will be stronger and have more endurance. Don't do it to fit in with others.

When you set out to make changes for yourself and not for your friends or your parents or your love interests, those changes are more likely to stick. When you are doing it for you and nobody else, you are internally motivated. When you try to make changes for others, you are externally motivated. Placing your self-esteem and self-worth in the hands of another means you must rely on that person's approval to keep you going. If he or she doesn't give you the encouragement and support you hoped for, you run the risk of giving up. *Why bother making such efforts to improve myself if so-and-so doesn't even appreciate them?* When you make those same efforts for yourself only, you only need to look within to see if you like the results. You only need to prove to *you* that you have done a good job, are doing better in school, or are getting stronger. When you do it for you, you always succeed.

Do You Like It?

My whole life has been a struggle for acceptance. I have constantly asked myself, *If I do this, will it make someone else think I'm good, think I'm worthy, think I'm charming, smart, or funny?* Most of what I have strived to achieve was for the benefit of hearing someone else say, "Good job." It didn't really matter who — mostly my parents, but it branched out into the realm of friends, boyfriends, and complete strangers, too. It was, and truthfully still is, a constant battle for me.

I went to college because I wanted to go. I also went because I thought that going would be something that would finally prove to others that I was worthy of their love and support. But I didn't believe in myself. I was scared I'd be revealed for the fraud I was — that someone would figure out that I didn't belong at this institution of higher education. They would throw me out and that would prove it. Prove I'm not worthy. Prove I'm not good enough. Prove I'm not smart enough. That was what I told myself every day.

In my junior year of college, I was offered a job as a teaching assistant for a class of sixteen preschool-age children. The school was based on the arts, a subject I loved, and I always had a deep affection for children. So I took the job. On my very first day, the teacher I was assisting told me, "We try not to tell the children 'good job.' If they ask you if you like something, turn the question back around on them and ask if *they* like it." I was puzzled. I thought children needed positive reinforcement. So I asked her why.

She looked at me and smiled as she explained, "Because we want *them* to like it. We want them to like themselves, to find joy in what they have done because it is their work. We are trying to build their self-esteem from within."

At first this notion puzzled me. No one had ever asked me if I liked what I had done or if I was proud of myself. This whole idea was new to me. So I tried it. I asked a little girl in the class if *she* liked her painting. She looked up at me and said, "I love it." I couldn't believe it. This four-year-old had achieved something that I hadn't. She loved her work because she loved herself. She loved something she did without needing outside reassurance or approval. Wow!

I returned home for the summer and decided that I wanted to buy a car. I was going to work, save my money, and buy it. In the back of my mind I was laughing at myself. *Yeah, right! You think you can get a job and earn enough money to pay for a car?* I dared myself to try it. I worked every day as a nanny. I worked, and waited for my parents, my friends, anyone to praise me. *Look at how hard I'm working! Look at what a good job I'm doing!*

At the end of the summer I walked into a car dealership and walked out with keys to my new car in hand. I had achieved my goal. My family and friends showered me with praise. It felt nice, but it wasn't as gratifying as I had expected.

After a few weeks, I knew what I had to do. As cheesy as it was, I knew it was necessary. I was sitting in my car and I looked at myself in the rearview mirror and asked myself, "Do *you* like it? Do you feel good?" I was asking myself if I was proud of what I had done, proud of my hard work and what I had achieved. And I was. I looked back at my reflection and yelled out loud, "Yes, I LOVE it."

Lia Gay

Daring to Dance

I'm a sixteen-year-old girl who has been struggling with anorexia for about six months. I have always watched what I ate, and body image issues have always seemed to be at the forefront of my consciousness. I'm a dancer so I am very in touch with my body and how I want it to look to the outside world.

This summer I took things to the extreme. I went to summer camp at a pretty low weight and I returned home weighing even less. I was weak, pale, and exhausted. My clothes were falling off, my fingernails turned yellow, and my hair was dry and dull. I was constantly freezing and would wear sweatshirts on hot summer days. The problem was, I didn't see a problem. I didn't realize how much weight I was losing or how much damage had been done.

At least somebody else was able to read the silent signals my body was sending out. About a week before camp was ending, some of the counselors noticed a problem and called my parents. Nobody thought it was life-threatening, so I wasn't sent home. But my parents scheduled a doctor's appointment for the day I returned.

When my parents picked me up from camp, I saw the shocked looks on their faces. At the doctor's office, I was given all sorts of tests, and blood work was done. My vital signs were so low my doctor wanted me admitted to the hospital immediately. I had never seen my father cry before. Seeing my father's tears for the first time made me realize what I had done to myself — and to my family.

I was in the hospital for six long days. The experience was perhaps the worst and best thing that ever happened to me. I was on strict bed rest and was hooked up to a heart monitor, which would start beeping when my heart rate dropped. The staff was strict. I had thirty minutes to eat my entire meal. If I didn't finish it, I would have to be force fed, meaning with a tube down my throat. The first time that happened, I decided I never wanted to go through that pain again, so I did something that was even more difficult for me. I ate.

The first night, the doctors told me they would start the portions out small and slowly increase them. Compared to what I was used to eating, the meal they served seemed like a gluttonous feast. I struggled to get it down. The tears were flowing, and I could feel myself getting fat. Each day they increased my food intake, and each day it got a little bit easier to eat. It was difficult being monitored and probed by a constant stream of doctors, nurses, nutritionists, and counselors, but in the end these visits made all the difference. Over the course of six days, these professionals intervened to save my life.

Once out of the hospital, the real challenge began: I was on my own. I had to follow a strict meal plan and keep any physical exertion to a minimum. I didn't realize how much I missed being physically active until I wasn't allowed to be. I missed being able to dance. And I missed how good my body felt when I danced. That gave me the encouragement to work hard to get my strength, and my self, back.

With the support of my family and friends and a sense of humor and humility about the whole process, I feel emotionally stronger with each passing day. I know that I have to stay on top of my eating habits and seek outside support when I am feeling vulnerable. But I'm dancing again. And I have realized that I may not always dance through life with grace and ease, but if I keep on dancing, I'll find my own rhythm.

Brenna Cipley

Model Daughter

When I was eleven years old, my mother bought me my first magazine subscription. It wasn't a subscription to *Girl's Life* or *Seventeen*, which other girls my age were thumbing through. It was *Vogue*. It was a little ahead of my time, but boy was I excited. I was reading a real woman's magazine!

After devouring the first two issues, I was convinced the *Vogue* lifestyle was the one for me. I became delighted at the thoughts of money, leisure, beauty, fame, and fashion. I learned about lingerie, crash diets, and makeup tricks — everything an eleven-year-old needs to know. Right? Well, maybe not.

I became fascinated with the people in the pages of the magazine. *They* looked important. *They* lived the lifestyle. I tried my hardest to emulate what I saw every month, and at the end of the year my mom renewed my subscription.

Barely even twelve years old, I felt like a woman trapped in the body of a little girl. I couldn't wait to jump into the world with all of the information I had attained over the year. But how to break out of my preteen existence? Yes, of course: modeling.

My mother was thrilled with the idea. She called photographers and agents all over the area. "Half Japanese, half Scandinavian, what a mix!" they would say. By the time I was thirteen, I had an agent and a hefty modeling portfolio. Although there

115

was a bit of concern over my height, my mother reassured them that I would grow.

But I didn't grow. I wasn't tall enough. My mother was wrong and I felt horrible. Every audition I walked into, I would leave rejected. When I finally booked a job for a swimsuit calendar, I began to feel pressure about my weight. I wasn't as tall as the other girls, and in turn I didn't look as thin.

I became hopelessly frustrated. I wanted to be taller. I wanted to be thinner. I wanted the *Vogue* lifestyle and I knew that my mother wanted it for me, too. At fourteen, I should have been concerned with friends and boys and school. Instead I spent my energy feeling inadequate, insecure, and confused. My self-esteem plummeted until I was writhing in self-hatred.

My mother didn't help the situation. She kept the pressure in high gear, keeping a close watch on what I was eating and how much I was exercising. She even sat me down one day and taught me how to smile the *right* way. Even my smile wasn't good enough.

The pressure was killing me. By the time I was sixteen, I had found a way to rid myself of guilt after eating. I would just throw up. I was relieved to have found a way to maintain the figure my mother wanted. I finally had some control over my life. At least I thought so at the time. I began to lose more and more weight until one of my teachers called my parents and expressed her concern. I was forced to admit that I had a problem. My mother was disappointed in me and refused to take any responsibility for *my* problem.

I didn't want this problem. I was tired of loathing my appearance. I was sick to death of hating myself. I wanted to get better. I began to attend eating disorder meetings, and I met other girls who knew what I was going through, other girls who had been there, too.

As I grew into a young adult, I found ways to value myself outside of my appearance. I knew that even if I would never be good enough for my mother, I was good enough for myself. I had more to offer the world than *Vogue* and bikini calendars. I realized that the *Vogue* lifestyle I so coveted wasn't a real life, at least not for me. I also realized that it's okay to have insecurities, as long as we keep them from defining us. By accepting the truth I was finally able to see and understand the real me: a strong and beautiful young woman who endured pressure and came out the other end a solid individual.

Even if I was never the model daughter my mother dreamed I would be, I am happy, and I know deep down that's really what she wanted for me all along.

Miya Goodrich

Learn from Your Pain

*Growing is a lifetime job, and we grow most
when we're down in the valleys, where the fertilizer is.*

Barbara Johnson

Learn from Your Pain

Nobody likes pain. Let's face it, it hurts. If you knew ahead of time the things that were going to cause you pain, you probably wouldn't do them. Although we avoid pain and often do our best not to feel it, pain is one of our greatest teachers.

How do children learn not to touch a hot stove? They do it once, feel the pain, and remember not to do it again. There are some points in life when you don't learn the first time and you have to experience the pain a couple of times before you get it. But like the child who stops touching the stove, if you can learn from your pain the first time you get hurt, you won't have to keep making the same mistakes over and over again.

You don't study for an upcoming test because you don't feel like it. What's the big deal? But when you get the test back with a bad grade, you understand. It doesn't feel good to get a low grade, especially when you know you could have done better if you had tried. The next time, you will probably study.

You talk about a friend behind her back. You repeat private things she has told you. She finds out. When you get her phone call and hear how angry she is, it feels bad. Then she starts crying and it feels *really* bad. Next time you will think twice about betraying the confidence of a friend. Pain teaches.

When you find yourself upset, brokenhearted, or suffering,

121

take the time to figure out the lesson behind the pain. Write about it in your journal or discuss it with a friend. Do whatever it takes to learn from your pain. Then, hopefully, you won't have to go through it again.

Down the Rabbit Hole

*In another moment down went Alice after it, never once
considering how in the world she was going to get out again.
There were doors all 'round the hall, but they were all locked,
and when Alice had been all the way down one side and up the
other, trying every door, she walked sadly down the middle,
wondering how she was ever to get out again.*

Lewis Carroll

"You've ruined everything. You gave in. You're weak," I whis-
pered fiercely. The eyes in the mirror filled with tears. I looked
away from her, allowing her the space to cry. My eyes fell on the
door to the handicapped stall of the stark bathroom. I walked
slowly toward it, wiping my eyes on my sleeve. I took a fateful
step into that stall, and tumbled down the rabbit hole.

I shut the door and slid the lock into place. I looked cau-
tiously at the white porcelain toilet and pushed the sleeves of my
shirt up to my elbows. Lifting the seat, I took a deep breath. I
opened my mouth as wide as I could.

I gagged and choked. Listening to the echo of my retching,
I gasped for breath. Bile stung my tongue, and my eyes began to
water. The acrid smell of vomit pervaded my nostrils, but I continued as if in a dream.

The door creaked. I froze, terrified that I would be caught. Spinning around so my feet faced the right way, my heart pounded as I listened to the intruder enter the stall next to mine. I listened, petrified, as she flushed the toilet and unlocked the door. I heard the water in the sink begin to run, the hand dryer start, and finally the creak of the door signaling her exit. I turned around and began again. The stomach acid was bitter in the back of my mouth. I watched as the last of my gluttonous dinner joined the revolting mixture already present.

When there was nothing left in my stomach, I realized I'd done all I could do. I looked at the undigested food that filled the bowl and was struck by an intense feeling of pleasure. I felt clean. Empty. I had regained control.

I pushed the shiny silver handle, lowered the seat, and left the stall. Once again, I examined my face in the mirror: eyes watering and puffy, nose running, a twisted smile. I scrubbed my reeking hands with soap, then used them to cup water and rinse out my mouth. I held my hands briefly beneath the dryer, acutely aware that I had been in the bathroom for a long time.

That Friday night, I crossed a line. My New Year's resolution had ceased to be a diet and had now become a disease. It progressed rapidly. I ate less and less, and vomited more with each passing week. I felt weak and was plagued by headaches. I didn't care. I was losing weight.

I categorized food into safe and unsafe groups. Some of the groupings were logical, but others were completely arbitrary. As time passed, more and more foods became unsafe. I was constantly tired but could not sleep at night. My hair pulled away from my scalp as I washed it in the morning. I bruised easily and felt cold all the time. Headaches tormented me daily. Standing up too quickly left me dizzy, and my pulse plodded along stubbornly.

Worse than the physical pain, however, was the emotional and mental anguish. I could not concentrate since I thought incessantly of food. During class, instead of listening to lectures or taking notes, I thought about what I had eaten that day, when I would eat again, what I would eat, and whether or not I would have the opportunity to throw up. I baked nightly and brought the treats to school the next day, distributing them among my friends. I watched others eat, vicariously savoring each bite. I read cookbooks and hoarded recipes. I never looked in the mirror without thinking, *fat*. I saw so much lard on my 5'2" frame that I was genuinely shocked when people said I was getting too thin. I weighed myself all the time. I thought of nothing but how I needed to be thinner. Eating unsafe food sent me flying to the nearest bathroom, slamming the door, and making myself throw up.

By the time I had lost a considerable amount of weight, it was fairly obvious that something was wrong. My friends had long ago expressed irritation at my constant nutrition monologues and excuses as to why I would not eat lunch. They began to confront me, threatening to go to the school counselors or to my parents. I told them to stay out of it, that I was fine, that I was in control. Finally, someone tattled. A friend called my mother and informed her of my behavior. My mother caught me vomiting two days later, and I was sent to therapy.

It took nine months of counseling before things started to improve. I gained back some weight along with the knowledge that I had been committing a slow suicide by starving my body in order to repent for what I considered an imperfect soul. I learned the difference between what I saw in the mirror and what was actually there. Though I have made significant advances, I know I still have work to do. I am still tortured by the voice in my head that tells me, "You're weak. You don't deserve that. You're useless, and you're alone in the world." It takes a great deal of strength for me to quiet her and to tell her that I will not careen headfirst down the rabbit hole again.

Stephanie Mayer

Spent

I have spent too many years,
staring into the mirror on the wall,
which only magnifies the imperfection,
back to my smiling face.

I have spent too many days,
trying to be the pillar of optimism,
that keeps up the facade,
even when everything's not okay.

I have spent too many nights,
covering up my tears and pain,
with an insecurity blanket made
of laughter and lies.

I have spent too many hours,
watching those carefree girls who
reflect the perfection of female beauty,
which I will never have.

I have spent too much time,
stepping up onto a scale,

only to measure my inability
to succeed at the smallest goals.

I have spent almost nineteen years,
living in this world,
and just now I'm beginning to wonder,
if I have ever really lived at all.

Kathryn Litzenberger

A Second Chance

The night my world came crashing down my mom was there to watch. I was nineteen years old with a death wish. My life up until this night had been filled with trauma and tragedy. At the early age of two I was raped, and when I was eleven, I was molested. At school I was teased and called horrible names by all the girls. I began to believe that I was a slut, a girl with nothing to offer but her body. I can't remember a time when there wasn't a boy attached to my side, until now.

I grew into an angry, vicious, depressed girl, emotionally stunted at the level of a two-year-old. I hated my life and everyone who was in it. I blamed my mother for my rape. I blamed her for my twisted ways. I told her she ought to be embarrassed and ashamed to show her face in public because she wasn't fit or worthy of the name "Mother." I lashed out at the world. Those who loved me the most got the the worst treatment. I hated them, but I hated myself most of all.

I fell in love with the poisons of the world. Drugs, alcohol, and sex became my escape. With each new day, my life became darker and more corrupt.

So at nineteen, I swallowed a bottle of pills. My mom opened the bathroom door just in time to pull the second bottle out of my hand. Suicide wasn't a stranger to me, either; my first attempt had occurred when I was ten years old.

An ambulance was called and I was rushed to the hospital. I threw up the black charcoal mix the nurses gave me so that the drugs inside of me could be released. My mom stayed with me the whole night.

Within a week, my bags were packed and I was admitted to an intensive therapy program. Twenty-four hours a day, seven days a week, for three months I had nowhere to look, except at myself. Each day was pure hell. I faced my worst demons behind those walls. I saw the animal I had become. For the first time, I experienced my family's pain; the pain *I* had caused them.

I am healing and the pain has eased up. I can acknowledge that I am human with human feelings. I now share those feelings with my parents and my friends. I am aware of others' lives and their feelings, and I am able to feel compassion and love in listening to their stories.

I cry because I still feel the shame of my past life. But I also cry happy tears because of the amazing love that is all around me. For the first time, the blinders are gone. I am now able to see the good things in my life. I never want to go back to that walking shell of a body — lifeless and dead.

With each new day, I wake with the desire to live. I ask myself, *What is in store for me today? Where is life going to take me today?* I choose who I want to be. I choose what I want for myself. My name is Tawnya Haynes. I am twenty years old, and I am happy to be me today.

Tawnya Haynes

Mirror Me

When I stare into the mirror,
What is it I see?
I see my own reflection,
Staring back at me.

But then I look deep within,
The mirror of my soul.
I see my present, and my past,
And what the future holds.

I see myself as what I am,
And what I could have been.
I see the shadow side of me,
That's hidden deep within.

As I stare at my reflection,
Staring back through my own eyes.
I see myself as others do,
But I also see the lies.

Others cannot see, of course,
This person I conceal.

They know the person I've become,
But my other side is real.

The mirror rids me of disguise,
Of hatred, truth, and tears,
I see myself through my own eyes,
And see my deepest fears.

Maybe I should end it all,
So many ways to die.
I lean up against my wall,
And suddenly begin to cry.

The tears stream down my face,
As I begin to say good-bye.
Good-bye, sunshine, good-bye, Mom,
Can't say I didn't try.

Then I look into the mirror,
And see me standing there.
A troubled, lost, and lonely child,
With tearstained cheeks and matted hair.

The mirror has two faces,
One of truth, reality.
The other is what others see,
My made-up fantasy.

Well, mirror, thanks for being there,
But it's time I step away.
It's time my mask came off for good,
The real me's here to stay.

Michelle M. Argueta

Touching Bottom

One afternoon in October, I walked into Keane Studios with my mom and brother to look at my senior pictures. The pictures had already been taken and this was just a review session for me to pick out which ones I actually wanted to buy. My mom, brother, an employee of the studio, and I all stuffed into a little room and suddenly pictures of me were covering the desk in front of us. I had to narrow the pictures down and, with my family's help, I narrowed them down to three.

Throughout the viewing session, my mom and brother kept making comments like, "Wow. Look, she's smiling," or, "Oh my gosh, I never knew she had teeth!" I just rolled my eyes at them and tried not to think about the implications of what they were saying. Eventually, though, even the employee decided to get into the act and she looked at me, all the while laughing and smiling, and said, "I take it you're not normally a happy person."

This comment stunned me for a second. This was a woman whom I had never met before, and with whom I had never had an intimate conversation. All she had done was spend fifteen minutes with my family and me. Yet she was able to sum up the essence of my life in her simple nine-word sentence.

Like many teenagers, it seemed that when I hit high school my moods and attitude took a nosedive into a sea of depression.

Unlike most kids, I needed a life preserver to ensure that I didn't drown. My life preserver finally came to me the summer between my sophomore and junior years. My therapist of almost a year, recognizing the need for some action besides talking to keep me afloat, decided that medication was my next best option. She put me on an antidepressant.

Though this pill seemed like the answer to my prayers, I was at first reluctant to accept it as the solution to my problems. To take a pill for depression meant that I had something chemically wrong inside of me, and I just wasn't ready to face that possibility. That meant that there was something wrong with me, something that made me different from all the other kids at school. So, like the million other times that I had done so, I cried in my therapist's office, feeling like the dejected teenager that I faced in the mirror every day.

It took some time, but the idea of taking medication eventually began to grow on me. I would ask myself questions like, *What if I could be happy? What would it feel like to be normal?* Eventually I stopped looking at the medication as a validation of a flaw in myself, but rather as a chance to improve my life. Before I knew it, a small medication container had found a permanent home on the nightstand next to my bed.

I take an antidepressant every night before I go to sleep. This pill doesn't make me happy. It doesn't make me want to smile all the time or break out in song at the beginning of the day. The medication keeps my moods level; it lets me think rationally. No storm clouds are stationed above my head.

I still have problems. I still cry on occasion and have horrible days when I don't want to talk to anyone. I have days when I wonder if my medication is even working. I've learned, though, that these dark days that no one ever wants to face are part of life; they are a part of growing up. Everyone has had their heart broken by someone before or been pushed aside by their best friend. What made me different from the common teenager was that I needed help beyond what my friends and family could offer.

I still see my therapist once a week. She never judges me or puts me down; she just listens. I've been lucky enough to find new friends since I started taking the medication — friends who listen and help me through the tough times. It is amazing what the power of love can do for someone.

Now when I look in the mirror, I see a completely different person. Before, I used to see the medication as evidence of a weakness in myself, but now I see it as something that has made me stronger. Many people have problems that need to be more carefully examined. I had the intelligence to realize when I was in trouble, and the courage to ask for help. I fight every day to make a better life for myself, and since life has already thrown this curveball at me, I feel I have had to work twice as hard as others. I'm not bitter about this, though, for I love who I've become and I love the challenge of life. And when things get really tough, I know that I can survive through the rough waters because I've done it before. If you look at my sea of depression now you won't see it completely dried up, but you'll notice my feet can touch the bottom — and that's all I've ever asked for.

Kameron Becker

As You Grow

When the broken hearts are mended and the many tears are dried, you learn. When you're over the old boyfriends and girlfriends and you realize you can live without your first love, you learn. You see that the world doesn't end just because you think it will, and that sometimes growing up means letting go. You learn what real love is, and you begin to see that one friend who really cares about you is better than a hundred friends who don't. You learn that you can be strong, take each day step-by-step, and survive every sad moment. So feel the pain and cry the tears, go out and experience life. But when you're at the end of your rope, and you're ready to jump off that ledge, remember that heartache fades, pain subsides, and though life seems at times too tough to handle, it's also too precious a gift to waste. Keep on living, never give up, and remember: As you grow, you learn.

Carrie Ann Bakley

Accept the Good and the Bad

Since every failure is a lesson, every challenge an opportunity,
and every joy a triumph, it's hard to go wrong.

Michael Addison Reed

Accept the Good and the Bad

In order to love yourself, or anyone else, you have to acknowledge that nobody is perfect. We all have traits or qualities that we would rather not have — and often choose not to accept.

For example, you might think it's bad that you are too sensitive. You might be ashamed that you cry frequently or that your feelings are hurt easily. Another person might look at your sensitivity as a good quality. It means that you are probably very tuned in to other people's feelings and that you often provide a nurturing shoulder to cry on. People who are highly sensitive usually have compassion and empathy for their friends.

You might get upset with yourself for being shy. You can never seem to get up the nerve to talk to that cute guy in your math class. That's okay — maybe he's shy, too! Some boys like girls who are quiet and reserved. Certainly it is good to speak up when you have something to say, but remember, everyone has his or her own style. You don't have to be standing at the top of the cheerleading pyramid to get your point across.

Though it may seem hard, you can learn to accept the things you don't like about your appearance. If you consider yourself too tall, for instance, instead of thinking of your height as a bad thing, look at the positive aspects. Clothes probably look good on you. You may have long legs that help you to run fast. You can see the stage at a crowded concert.

If you're upset because your once smooth skin now appears covered with pimples, remember: Many teenagers have various degrees of acne. Your skin probably doesn't look as bad to others as it does to you. In all likelihood, once you've gone through puberty, your skin will clear up. Picking at your skin won't make it look better, and getting upset about it won't make you feel better. Accepting that your body is going through natural changes right now, and that your skin problems probably won't last forever, will.

There is light and dark; people laugh and cry. This is what makes life so full. Next time you are not accepting all aspects of yourself, just remember that there are two sides to every coin. What bothers you about yourself today may be what you like best about yourself tomorrow.

Once I Was a Flower

Once I was a flower,
But now I'm just a stem.
I didn't like my petals
So I did away with them.

I thought my colors ugly,
So I threw them all away.
Wanted orange, red, and purple.
Didn't like my shades of gray.

To look like other flowers was all I really wanted,
Like all the other roses who were never teased and taunted.
Like the child who's picked last for elementary school athletics,
I thought that I was worthless and I blamed it on genetics.

I wanted to be chosen for a beautiful bouquet,
But I knew no one would want me for my ugly color gray.
So I tore my petals out and I threw them to the ground,
With the wind they blew away and were never to be found.

Now I stand here naked with all my petals gone for good,
And I wish that long ago I would have only understood
That looks can be deceiving and that gray is not so bad.
Now I know that I possessed more than I thought I had.

Danielle Rosenblatt

Pinocchio

I have a big nose, and I'm no longer ashamed to admit it.

Up until the beginning of sixth grade, I was completely and totally unaware of my affliction. Although I come from a family with a tendency toward prominent noses, I had always mistakenly believed that I had been spared this particular familial trait. What can I say? I was naive. And because nobody had ever mentioned my nose to me before, I'd had no reason to think that it was anything out of the ordinary.

Then I entered middle school, a world mired in pretense and superficiality. Middle school is where dolls and make-believe begin to lose their appeal to girls hovering on the threshold of adolescence — and where outward appearances become of the utmost importance. During these years, rapidly changing ways of thinking lead many to value one thing above all others: uniformity. Those who appear different in any way are often singled out and picked on mercilessly, and I was no exception.

I still remember the day clearly. It was fifth-period lunch and I sat at my usual table in the cafeteria, munching away on a sandwich and discussing some trivial matter with my friends. Suddenly, a shrill voice rang out from a lunch table to our right: "Hey, Pinocchio!"

Startled, I turned my head to face the voice. Several girls considered popular at the time stared back at me, their eyes glinting and their mouths twisted into cruel smiles.

"Are you talking to me?" I sputtered, unsure of what they could possibly mean by calling me "Pinocchio."

The girl who struck me as the leader of the pack nodded, the irksome smugness never leaving her face. "Boy, I'm glad I don't have your schnoz!" she giggled. Her friends giggled, too — irritatingly high-pitched squawks that sent the blood rushing into my face. I could feel my cheeks heating up and I knew, just knew, that I was bright red. Unwilling to let them feast upon my humiliation, I quickly turned away from their table to face my friends.

"What are they talking about?" I exploded in as hushed a manner as I could manage. "I don't have a big nose! Why are they calling me Pinocchio?"

That's when I noticed that Maya was avoiding my gaze.

"M-Maya? I don't have a big nose . . . right?"

Maya glanced at our other friends, who were also trying a bit too hard not to look me directly in the face. "No, you don't have a big nose. Not exactly, anyway," she hedged, obviously choosing her words very carefully.

"What do you mean, 'not exactly'?" I demanded.

"Well, I mean, your nose isn't exactly small. But I'm not saying it's big! No, it's not big. It's probably just, uh, more prominent than those girls are used to."

After that incident — which seems so minor in retrospect — my entire world and everything I'd thought I understood within it seemed to collapse around me. Each morning I would rise from bed and head straight for the bathroom, where I would scrutinize my nose critically in the three-way mirror. I examined it from all angles, tracing it with one finger and even going so far as to outline its shape onto the glass using my mother's red lipstick. It took me a couple of weeks to come to terms with the fact that I was indeed in possession of a big nose.

The taunts of "Pinocchio" continued for months, and although I tried as best as I could to ignore them, they stabbed straight into my soul. To my sixth-grade mind, it just wasn't fair. Why should everyone else get perky little ski-jump noses while I was stuck with this . . . this . . . *monstrosity* in the middle of my face?

For the next several years, my nose served as my number-one source of humiliation. Although the "Pinocchio" joke eventually wore thin and died out, my lack of confidence remained alive and kicking. I'd cringe whenever I flipped through a photo album because I felt that I looked like a freak. In almost every picture I'd be flanked by friends with dainty little noses, or, at the very worst, noses that were long but straight and unobtrusive. Meanwhile, my nose — with its flaring nostrils and bump in the middle — seemed to stand out as some sort of beacon, announcing, "Look, everybody! Here's Marisa, the girl with the huge nose!" My mother kept insisting that my nose was perfect, but I refused to believe her or even to listen to her reassuring words.

I'm in college now, and I'd be lying if I said that my nose never bothers me anymore. Most of my close friends, both from home and from school, have heard me complain about it or at least crack jokes about it, and I still occasionally take a few minutes to stop and examine my nose in the mirror. But more often than not I don't think twice about it. This is mainly due to my discovery of a world beyond middle school — a world where outward appearance is still important but where friendliness, talents, and personality take precedence over a lump of flesh between the eyes and mouth. My first year at college was especially crucial in shaping this discovery. Leaving all that was familiar, spending a year in a totally new place, and meeting new people helped me realize that not everyone is created from a cookie cutter and that not everyone *wants* to be. Sure, there will always be people for whom looks are more important than anything else, but the majority of people are willing to look beyond what they may consider physical shortcomings and appreciate others for who they truly are — especially because nearly everyone dislikes some aspect of their *own* outward appearance. Self-realization cannot be achieved and meaningful friendships cannot develop unless each of us learns to stop obsessing over how we, and others, look.

So the next time you see me waiting at a red light in my car, pull up beside me and call me "Pinocchio" if you really want. A few years ago the name would have injured my ego nearly beyond repair. Today, I will probably just look at you funny out the side window — then drive off toward the house of a friend who values me for the creative, friendly, prominently nosed girl I am.

Marisa S. Hoheb

Beautiful All Along

All I ever wished for was to be beautiful. Whenever I came across a wishing well, I would toss my coin in and wish for beauty. I wished upon shooting stars that I would wake up beautiful. And when I blew out the candles on my birthday cake, I wished that this would be the year that I became beautiful.

I couldn't look in the mirror without seeing something wrong with myself. My hair was wrong, my clothes didn't look right, and I just couldn't get my makeup to improve my face. I was depressed, sad, and disappointed with myself. I felt alone, like no one ever understood me. I hated my family, isolated myself, barely ever went out, and sometimes even wished I would die. After endless nights of crying myself to sleep, trying to run away from home, locking myself in my room, and being afraid to look at myself in the mirror, I knew something had to change.

For many years, I didn't realize that I was actually a beautiful person who had a lot going for herself. Eventually, I started to grow out of my awkward puberty stage and develop into a woman. I started taking better care of myself, and little by little my confidence grew. Suddenly it didn't matter as much what people thought of me. The girl who once blended in with the wall had matured, grown, and become wiser. People started noticing a difference, and I started interacting with others around me without wondering what they thought of me. I found my personal style and became comfortable with it. What I didn't know was that in order for everyone to think highly of me, I had to think highly of myself first.

This wasn't something that happened overnight. I still work on believing that I'm perfect just the way I am. I have ugly days and critique myself in the mirror; that's normal. But I have overcome the desire to be something I'm not. I won't be the next Marilyn Monroe or Julia Roberts, but that's okay because I'll be beautiful to me. I don't need to be accepted or loved by everyone around me. It is enough to simply accept and love myself.

Melissa Heitzman

Go Beyond Your Comfort Zone

And the trouble is, if you don't risk anything, you risk even more.

Erica Jong

Go Beyond Your Comfort Zone

Sometimes in order to grow, you need to step outside of your comfort zone. You need to do things that you normally would avoid doing because they make you feel uncomfortable or inadequate in some way.

A big challenge for me is taking classes in something I know nothing about. I don't like being in situations where I feel less than brilliant. One time I decided to learn martial arts. When I got to the class, it was filled with students who were at all different levels. Some had been studying for years while others had been in the class for only a month or so. I, however, was the only one who was there for the first time. Oh, joy! The teacher came over and taught me a move that involved shifting my weight from one foot to the other. After about five minutes of doing this, I was anxious to have him show me another move. Instead he looked at me and said, "Good job, just keep doing that for now." I had to do that seemingly simple move for the entire hour. I felt humiliated. Looking back I now see why it was so important. Almost everything in martial arts revolves around that move.

Physically, going beyond your comfort zone can include training for a marathon or lifting weights a few more times than usual. Emotionally, you sometimes have to push yourself to leave the house and go out even when you feel too depressed to do so. Or you have to face something that you'd rather not deal with — like talking to your teacher about your grades or confronting a friend who has done something that upset you.

When considering going beyond your comfort zone, be sure to pay attention to your instincts. For example, don't do things with your boyfriend that you're not ready to do, no matter what. Don't do anything that is harmful or scary to you. There is sometimes a fine line between what you should or shouldn't do. For instance, if all your friends are going jet-skiing and your instinct tells you to sit on the beach with a book, then I would suggest sitting on the beach. Jet-skiing probably isn't dangerous, but if you don't feel right about it, don't do it. However, if you have been sad about a fight you had with your boyfriend and your friends invite you out to see a movie with them, this might be an excellent idea. When it comes to going beyond what is comfortable, always listen to your inner voice and let it guide you.

Everybody's comfort zone is different. Only you know what yours is and what it means to go beyond it. You know when life presents you with a chance to stretch and grow. Next time a positive opportunity arises, go for it. You will feel better for doing so. Talk to the new girl in school or sign up for a dance class. Stepping outside your comfort zone builds inner strength and character. It gives you the awareness that you can do new things and face tough challenges.

The Girl

Many years from now when my skin has deep wrinkles and my memory has some missing links, I will recall my days as a young girl, naive adolescent, lost twenty-something, proud parent, and inquisitive elder. When questioned by children and grandchildren as to whether or not I lived my life to the fullest, I will ask, "Have you ever heard of Outward Bound?"

It was this leadership seminar (described more accurately by veterans as "a monthlong, backbreaking, feet-blistering, finger-numbing, mind-blowing, soul-searching battle to the bloody end") that verified my participation in the ceremony of life. For twenty-three days I removed my watch and headphones, marked the sun at high noon, and listened to the canyons sing. I swam down rapids, rappelled over 200-foot cliffs, and declared my intention to annihilate the local insect population. I migrated among herds of sheep and walked the path of the mountain lion. I outsmarted loose rocks and crossed rivers without saturating the soles of my boots.

I embraced my endorphin supply with a gratitude I had never known before. I was introduced to every muscle and tendon in my five-foot, eleven-inch frame. I felt an acute burning in my calves as I methodically ascended 14,000-foot mountain peaks. Soon, however, the distress was no longer a physical imposition. Five days of carrying an eighty-pound backpack jump-started my idle muscles. Paddling for eight hours straight became natural and routine. Pain that had once settled inside my body now stood up and walked down my legs to my ankles, slid out the tips of my toes, and crawled to a tiny creek where it flowed to the sea and was lost on the horizon.

The urge to bathe gradually faded. After five days I braided my hair for the last time and used my hairbrush as a dish cleaner for the remainder of the trip. My comrades and I began emitting a stench I imagined most intolerable to those unaccustomed to a soap-free lifestyle. We laughed and claimed we smelled like roses. We *did* smell like roses — roses wilted from overexposure to sweat, mixed with sunscreen and bug repellent.

I slowly forgot what I looked like. I ignored the outline of my body quivering on lake surfaces and turned from my own reflection in others' sunglasses. I became a mental mosaic — a combination of the features of those with whom I traveled. I watched my feet, alarmed yet satisfied, as they became saturated with calluses and blisters, my toenails yellow and crusted with dirt.

At one point I misplaced the better part of my mental reasoning. The solo experience (being left alone in the wilderness with water as one's only source of nourishment) was meant to allow time for recuperation, deep thought, and reflection. The moon surely laughed as I lay lifeless in the heart of the forest, jacket half-zipped and one pant leg rolled up to the kneecap. An ant slowly scaled the length of my arm, pausing at the elbow. I did not have the energy to brush it away. A strand of hair stuck to my left cheek, and when I closed my eyes, my body pressed against the rocky floor. My fingertips and toes grew roots as I sunk into the earth, gazing in a catatonic stupor at the heavens above.

I hiked for days without trails, paddled when I was too sore to move, and pressed on. I drank stream water purified with iodine and ate homemade snow cones topped with cheap sports drink powder. I ate only peanut butter for twenty-three days straight. I felt more alive than I ever had in my sixteen years of self-conscious existence.

I unlearned how to be a girl. I thought of friends back home and saw that one possessed an unwavering inability to make a decision. I thought about another's obsession with looks and material possessions. I thought of a friend who couldn't run a mile without getting a sideache. I looked down at the hair growing on my legs and swore that never again would I own a razor. After all, I could carry as much as the boys, catch and kill mosquitoes with my bare hands, and do fifty push-ups in a row without breaking a sweat. I would no longer, under any conditions whatsoever, wear a dress.

On the last day I ran, without stopping, for seven miles. Waiting at the finish line was a yellow school bus, my return ticket to civilization.

I shaved my legs. I wore a dress. Then I ate an entire bowl of ice cream because I liked the taste and not because I needed the energy. I cried when I saw my friends, deciding that the splendor of the natural world would never compare to my love for the people in my life.

Every so often, when the industrial world proves too much for my wild heart, I think of my twenty-three days spent in the middle of nowhere and remember the rush of standing on the highest mountaintop and being able to see for miles. I remember waking with the sun and sleeping with the moon. I remember collapsing on my backpack, gazing at the clouds, and listening to each individual beat of my human heart. I remember watching my chest rise and fall as the sweet air filled my belly; then exhaling, returning my breath to the greens of the mountains.

Given a choice, this girl would still give up her hairbrush and eat peanut butter for a week just to once again stare in awe at the mountaintops and wonder how high she could climb. And at the end of the climb would await the greatest gift: myself in the simplest of all possible forms — hungry, hairy, and real.

Chesney Kathryn Dougherty

Impulsive Identity

Make a wish upon an eyelash.
Kiss a butterfly.
Run barefoot over sandy beaches.
Blow dandelion seeds into the sky.

Make a statement loud and clear.
Say what's on your mind.
Wear whatever you want to wear.
Show the world you're undefined.

Run and play with wild horses.
Let your hair fly free.
Be confident. Express yourself.
Let no one tell you who to be.

Practice karate on a trampoline.
Be wild and dye your hair.
Laugh and sing at the top of your lungs.
Spread smiles everywhere.

Show everyone your fearless self.
Now's your time to shine.
Don't fear at all what others think.
Just paint your own design.

Kate Neely

Embrace Your Uniqueness

And so I sit and wait for the day,
When I can be seen in my own special way.
Just myself, how I should be;
Not at all perfect — just perfectly me.

Melissa Munro

Embrace Your Uniqueness

All of us are stars and deserve the right to twinkle.
Marilyn Monroe

We are all unique, different, one of a kind. Part of learning who we are is comparing ourselves to those around us. We all go through periods in our lives when we want to be like everyone else — or at least how we perceive others to be.

In high school I remember I had to have the same clothes, the same basic hairstyle, even the same set of values as my best friends. It made me feel safe. If I wore the same jeans, the same brands, and the same kind of shoes as everyone else, then I was sure to fit in. Or at least I wouldn't be making the mistake of standing out by wearing the wrong thing.

This is a normal part of growing up and, strangely enough, it is part of the process of finding your uniqueness. Just be sure you don't stop there. Once you have found a comfortable foundation for your appearance, it becomes safe to branch out and add things that are unique to you — the accessories you choose, the way you wear your hair, and many other details that contribute to your own unique style.

Of course, this doesn't only apply to how you look. It also applies to your personality and to an overall picture of who you are.

Once again, everybody is different. If you think about your friends and their differences, you can see how important it is that you aren't all the same. You might have one friend you rely on when you need advice. Another friend might be someone you love to laugh and be silly with. Yet another friend might be creative and the one you turn to when you want to do magazine collages or tie-dye shirts together. If all your friends were exactly the same, your life wouldn't be as rich as it is. This is another reason it is so important to embrace your uniqueness. Ask your friends what they like most about your friendship and how your uniqueness adds a special element to it. Allow yourself to be open to different music, new hobbies, and spontaneous adventures that might be fun and exciting.

Remember that you are similar to others, and yet you are different. The differences are the things that define you and give you a sense of who you are. These are the things that make you a special person.

Living in the Illusion

I am not perfect. I never have been and I never will be. I'm not blond, though my hair hasn't always been its original shade of brown, courtesy of Clairol and Sun-In. I'm 5'7", which means I will probably never be a world-class gymnast, but then again my inability to tumble would probably have been just as big an obstacle. I don't have a flawless figure. So modeling, or even squeezing into the clothes of Kate Moss and Tyra Banks, is totally out of the question. My feet are big, my complexion is flawed, my eyes are large, and my nails are short (because I bite them). In the summer I burn and freckle; I don't tan. I am neither petite nor elegant. I am far from fat-free, and my pockets are not brimming with funds to purchase the latest fashions. And in all honesty, I like it that way.

From the time I was old enough to know the difference between black and white, wrong and right, people would try to complicate things with the gray areas. For a long time everything had to be one or the other — good or bad, beautiful or ugly. I wasn't beautiful so I must have been ugly, and all my faults only made me uglier. With each new scar on my knee or imperfection that appeared on my face, I became more and more unattractive to myself. My friends were perfect. Their vibrant, blond, curly locks were much more pleasing to the eye than my thick, long, straight-as-a-whip brown hair — or so I believed. So since difference isn't cool when you're in elementary school, I took to conforming to the norm rather than establishing myself as an individual. If fluorescent pink was the color du jour, I was wearing it, even though I hated pink. If two inches of makeup on my face helped me resemble my stunning peers, then I became the Mary Kay poster girl no matter how much my pores screamed for mercy at night. If almost all the girls in my class had three earrings in each ear, I'd willingly let a licensed professional punch holes in my unsuspecting little lobes. I became a sort of clone — one of the countless young girls who was afraid to be themselves, knowing it may mean being different, and different is not normal.

But I was always different. No matter what I did, what I wore, what I said. I was distinct, dissimilar, unlike all my friends, as much as I attempted to become one of them. They did not always feel the same way I did. My face was not the same shape as theirs. I didn't fit the stereotypical physical mold of a woman. My body curved and slanted in different directions. My friends and I were totally distinct people with separate thoughts and appearances. Why on earth were we trying to look exactly alike? When I finally realized that, I also realized something else: I like myself just the way I am.

I am seventeen, 5'7", with light brown hair and bright blue eyes. I am not a small size and I never will be. My stomach is not concave, my breasts are not perfectly round and big, and, amazingly enough, I have hips. I can't hide or mask who I am. It's too hard and it takes more effort than I have the time with which to deal. In my opinion, I could be using that time for more important things. I am a straight-A high school student, on the honor roll, a member of our student council, and in countless other extracurricular activities. I write for the newspaper and am president of Students Against Drinking and Driving. I also hold down a job and am currently applying to numerous universities. Self-hatred is a waste of the little time I have to spend on myself.

I know people half my size and double my intellect who still have not discovered the gray area that lies between beauty and ugliness. They have yet to realize that beauty isn't achieved through fashion or makeup. It isn't achieved through the opinions of others. Beauty can be achieved in any form. It is possessed by all. It's just a matter of uncovering it.

Cheryl Amanda Gullage

So I'm Told

I am . . .
unspeakably loud,
insanely normal,
creatively dull,
horribly good,
arrogantly humble,
hysterically calm,
perfectly imperfect,
simply complex,
precisely off-center,
cynically optimistic,
foolishly realistic,
incompetently capable,
animatedly real,
patiently anxious,
cowardly courageous,
characteristically remarkable,
or so I'm told.
And I'm completely okay with it.

Megan Morris

I Am Beautiful

If everyone lit their own candle, the whole world would be lit.
Mary Moskovitz

I am beautiful.

I don't have a perfect complexion. I don't have an incredible smile or eyes that draw people in. I am 5'3", average by most standards, and I bite my nails. My makeup never looks quite right, and I get tiny nicks all over my legs when I shave. No one has ever accused me of being gorgeous.

But I am beautiful.

I see beauty everywhere. I see beauty in the eyes of a homeless person. I see beauty in my mother, even though she never wears makeup, has glasses dating from the early '80s, and can't be bothered reading magazines with the word "beauty" anywhere on the cover. She is gorgeous. I am able to see through to the soul of everyone.

I am beautiful.

I will never be a model, win a beauty pageant, or have my hands used in print ads. My feet are covered with scars left over from my eleven years of ballet, eleven years of trying to find beauty through flashy costumes, stage makeup, and hundreds of opening night roses. As it turns out, beauty wasn't to be found up onstage or in the applause of an audience.

But I am beautiful.

I see beauty in the world. I see beauty in my grandmother's eyes, even though they don't always recognize me since she developed Alzheimer's. I see beauty in my best friend's smile, even though he seeks truth through isolation.

I am beautiful.

I know that on the outside I wouldn't stop traffic, but I also know that if you dig a little deeper you will strike gold. I feel beautiful because I see beauty everywhere. By seeing beauty even in unlikely places, I am able to see the beauty in me. By seeing the beauty in me, I can't help but smile. And when I smile:

I am beautiful.

Andrea Maikovich

Practice Kindness

Kindness in words
Creates confidence
Kindness in thinking
Creates profoundness
Kindness in giving
Creates Love

Lao-tse

Practice Kindness

Nothing gets you out of a "poor me" mood faster than doing something kind for someone else. Whether you perform a community service or just smile at someone who looks like they need a smile — when you give to others, you feel better.

It is easy to focus your attention on wanting to be loved. Instead, try to recognize that when you give your love *away,* you also experience a wonderful feeling. I'm sure you can recall a time when you felt good after helping someone else.

An important part of life is learning how to give and receive love. Some of us feel more comfortable giving, while others are more comfortable receiving. But in order to experience love completely, we must learn to embrace both sides. It can be uncomfortable to be on the receiving end of kindness. You may feel indebted, or pressured to reciprocate right away, or just plain embarrassed. But you should let others do nice things for you and allow yourself to feel grateful. Kindness goes both ways — it is important to be kind to others and to let others be kind to you.

As girls, we are often taught to be nice, think of others, and not be selfish. Although these are good qualities, you also need to allow yourself to be upset, sad, or angry. It's okay to be in a bad mood. It's okay to feel down. It's okay to yell, argue, and cry. Be careful not to fall into the pattern of only wanting to be nice and never expressing your feelings when you have been let down or mistreated. Having self-respect means you acknowledge all of your emotions.

The next time you have been feeling down and are ready to feel better, try doing something for someone else and see how fast your mood changes. Tell your mom how grateful you are for all she does. Tell your best friend how important she is to you. Reach out to someone at school who looks like he or she could use a friend. Practicing kindness will make you feel happier. In giving to others, you give to yourself as well.

This is a prayer that I say at the beginning of each day to help me remember to practice kindness:

May I be happy
May I be peaceful
May I be free

May my friends be happy
May my friends be peaceful
May my friends be free

May my enemies be happy
May my enemies be peaceful
May my enemies be free

May all things be happy
May all things be peaceful
May all things be free

Buddhist prayer

Lullaby for Your Friend

When she's crying on your shoulder
And you don't know what to say.
Just whisper softly in her ear
That everything will be okay.
When she says her heart is broken
And her soul feels so alone,
Just tell her that you love her,
Just tell her on the phone.
When you hear her breathe so gently
And see tears fall from her eyes,
Wipe them one by one away,
Tell her everybody cries.
And soon she will look up at you
And maybe start to smile,
And thank you just for being there
Through all the painful while.
And you'll look down in her golden eyes,
And know just what to say:
That on you she can depend
And everything will be okay.

Rebecca Woolf

Be Grateful

All of us are lying in the gutter,
but some of us are looking up at the stars.

Oscar Wilde

Be Grateful

It is very easy to get caught up in thinking about all the things you don't have. You wish for a romantic relationship. You wish you were popular. You wish that your parents had more money so they could buy you a car for your sixteenth birthday. You waste an enormous amount of energy thinking about how much better things would be, if only. *If only I was taller or shorter. If only I was prettier, or thinner, or more muscular. If only my parents were cool, or rich, or nice, or still together. If only school was easier, or more fun, or nonexistent.*

When you spend all of your time thinking about what you don't have, you feel sad. When you spend time feeling grateful for the things you do have, you feel better. It really is that simple. Gratitude is a natural antidepressant.

Sometimes when I am feeling down and a bit less than grateful, I will make a list, either in my head or on paper, of all the things I have to be thankful for. It takes only a few minutes, and it completely changes my mood.

Life treats you differently when you approach it from a grateful place. Starting and ending each day thinking about the things you're grateful for will improve your attitude and your life.

When a friend thanks you for doing a favor for her, for helping her through a hard time, or for just being you, it makes you feel great. So when you are making your gratitude list, be sure your name is on it. Remember to be grateful for your abilities, for your personality, and most of all, be grateful that you are you.

Inspiration

It's so strange — life. Why some people are born and do nothing but suffer their whole lives. Poverty, pain, whatever the case is. And some people grow up with a life of luxury. I don't have a perfect life, but there's nothing I would change. I wish I could sit here and say I thank God every day for my blessings, but that would be a lie. I don't thank God nearly enough. When I think of people who are blind, I can't imagine going a day without seeing the sun come in through my window, or not being able to look into people's eyes when they speak. And then when I think of people who are deaf, I can't even begin to imagine what it would be like to not hear Derek say my name, or his sweet voice whispering, "Baby, I love you." I'm so very blessed, and I think most of us tend to take our blessings for granted. Of course, I wish some things were different. I wish I could weigh a little less, be a tad bit prettier, and have the newest clothes and the hippest music. I wish I could look at people and not judge them. I wish I could let my mom hug me once in a while. I wish I could go one day without sleeping in class. But unfortunately, we don't always get what we wish for, and I'm more than willing to settle for what I have.

Tonight, when I go to bed, I think I'll let my mom hug me and I'll tell her I love her. And I'll try to go to bed a little earlier, so maybe I won't be so tired and I can actually pay attention in history. And tomorrow, I'll eat a little healthier, I'll do my hair nice, and I'll take Gordy for a walk after school. Just to feel better about myself. And when I get home, I'll look in the mirror and tell myself that I am beautiful. Maybe next week, I'll go to the last dance of the year just to listen to the music a little more carefully and to look in people's eyes a little deeper than usual. After all, I have only one life to live, so I better make it good. And about this whole inspiration thing, if life itself isn't something to celebrate, I don't know what is.

Leighann Posey

I Am Grateful

One more block! I tell myself, as I feel my legs getting heavier, my arms swinging wildly in the air, my breath being sucked out by the wind of my movements. The sweat from my bangs rushes down my face, stinging my eyes, and warming my pounding heart. With each tree, each face, each car rushing past me, I feel more and more caught up in the blur of my neighborhood. Finally I slow to a stop as I land my feet on the familiar driveway and hear the curious bark of my neighbor's dog. I see my reflection in the rain puddle below, and I smile at the flushed cheeks, the dark almond eyes, and the messy ponytail — and I know that I am beautiful.

I believe beauty is in the eye of the beholder, and I know that that eye is my own. What makes me beautiful? I'm confident about what I can do while living in this world. I know what makes me happy, and I go for it. I wake up in the morning, laugh at my bad breath, and go brush my teeth. Many people are unsatisfied with their imperfections. When they try to do something new, they worry about failure. I know I will always have a 50/50 chance when it comes to trying something new, and after doing my best, making mistakes, and getting embarrassed once or twice, I continue to try. Confidence reflects beauty — if I'm true to myself, then I'm ready for others to be true to me.

I am beautiful because I have balance in my life; the inspirations that influence the person I am come from many different directions. I was born in China, where I lived up until I turned three. Afterward, I moved to Germany with my parents, and for five years I spent my nights sleeping next to the Swiss Alps and Lake Constance. Now I'm spending my teenage years growing up in American society. I feel like I understand three different worlds, cultures, and governments. When I look through old pictures of myself, slanting with the leaning tower of Pisa, waving by the Eiffel Tower, or simply reading under my homemade village of stars, I feel that those memories have made me the person I am today, the person that I find beautiful.

How do I know so many things about what makes a person beautiful? My parents have been my teachers, my providers, and my comfort throughout the years, and I am thankful for that. I am beautiful because they have given me a diverse life and lessons that my mind will possess every day when I wake up. My mom has taught me how to live a healthy lifestyle, cooking Chinese vegetable dishes for dinner, and my dad has raised me to love sports and politics. So when I tell you that I'm beautiful, it's mainly because the environment around me has made this way. I am grateful.

Win-Xi Wang

Set Boundaries

A "NO" uttered from the deepest conviction is better and greater than a "YES" merely uttered to please, or what is worse, to avoid trouble.

Mahatma Gandhi

Set Boundaries

Setting boundaries is never an easy thing to do. You may not like telling someone, "No, I can't help you with your homework right now because I need time for myself." Likewise, when it comes to setting boundaries on your own behavior, you may not like denying yourself an extra hour in the sun because it isn't good for your skin. But setting boundaries is something that becomes easier once you understand and experience the consequences of not taking care of yourself.

For instance, you can convince yourself to pass on your relaxation time, go to your friend's house, and help with her homework. You can rationalize that it's more important to do a good deed than to respond to your own needs. But if you make a habit of putting your friend's needs before your own, you will grow resentful. Your friendship may suffer. Similarly, it is easy to convince yourself that an extra hour outside won't hurt you. But the truth is, tan or no tan, your skin will be damaged by spending too much time in the sun. As you learn what is necessary for your well-being, you begin to set boundaries for yourself.

Small children feel safer when boundaries are set for them. They derive a sense of security from knowing what they can and cannot do. Even though you are older, the same holds true for you. If you know ahead of time what things you will and won't do, you will feel much more confident when you are in a decision-making situation. You can set boundaries concerning how you will allow people to treat you and how much you are willing to give in a friendship or romantic relationship, and the kinds of risks you are willing to take in general.

Setting boundaries and sticking to them is a challenge. But each time you do it and you experience how good it feels, it becomes easier. Remember: Your boundaries are your own. If you are firm in your convictions, other people's opinions cannot shake them. There might be those who try to get you to do things that feel wrong to you. But remember, the people who really love you and have your best interests at heart will respect your limits.

Once Upon a Time I Lost Myself

Sometimes we lose it. We fall into love like a pillowed net and lie there for months in LaLaLand. I've been there — in that net. I've been there countless times. It wasn't the first time or the last, but once upon a time I lost myself. He was the guy that I had watched from afar for months. His eyes drew me in from across the campus, the party, even the football game, and saturated my thoughts. He made me weak in the knees; he made me feel different.

When he finally asked me out, I was overjoyed. It felt as though everything I once questioned was suddenly defined. It was a wonderful moment, the first of its kind that actually lasted. We spent every afternoon together, every evening on the phone, every morning laughing at the bus stop.

On our three-month anniversary, he threw me a party. When we both showed up at the restaurant, our table for ten was empty. He had called my closest girlfriends, and not one of them showed up. We sat there in the darkness at a table much too big for two and had our anniversary alone. It didn't faze me that my friends hadn't showed up. It didn't matter that Billy and I were alone again. We were always alone and it felt good that way. I didn't even question the fact that my girlfriends had fallen off the planet. I couldn't see past my own two feet, I couldn't look ahead at the path paved only for two; there was no room for anyone else but Billy. We were a couple. We were in love, our names sewn from the same string.

Dreams fall apart sometimes. We wake up and everything is different.

One day I woke up, and the fantasy that Billy and I had created was torn, revealing the reality on the other side of the wall we had formed. It was easy to be idealistic about love; I had never felt this way about anybody. We had built a cocoon around each other, wanting nothing more but to become butterflies together — and here we were, flying away.

As I emerged from the darkness that morning, I realized that isolation wasn't the answer. I had pushed my friends and my family out of my life. I had thrown down the truth, hidden my identity, and dismissed the me that once was. I lost myself in his eyes, in his arms, and now who was I?

That afternoon I called Billy. The phone must have rung a hundred times. He wasn't there, though. He was gone. I knew he was. When I finally got ahold of Billy we agreed to meet at the bus stop, where we had met every morning during our days together.

I sat there in front of those blue eyes, the eyes that used to draw me in like tractor beams. The eyes that held me in, the eyes that made me forget my own. The eyes that now looked different. I told him that it was unfair for us both to continue to deprive ourselves of our lives. I told him that I missed my friends, and I missed being called Becca instead of the "Becca and Billy" that had become our joint title. I wanted to be together, but not all the time. I wanted to be in love, but not in exchange for my identity. I wanted to look into his eyes and see his eyes, without the glow of my own reflection. I didn't want to lose myself, and I feared I already had.

The lamppost shivered, and tears blurred us both from each other. The wind shifted and the light above us streamed down. Billy looked at me and smiled. He smiled and then he kissed my eyelids. He knew I was right. He told me so later, and although we stayed together only another three weeks, that night was the first time we truly understood what it meant to be in love. That was the first night we walked without stepping on each other's shadow. That was the first night I was Becca and he was Billy. Two names. Two souls. Two selves.

LaLaLand is overrated. I had been lost somewhere in a world where my identity wasn't necessary. I see that now. My friends and I have come together once again. We have forgiven each other for losing sight of our priorities, and ditching each other for our relationships. Billy and I still speak; we still talk about that night at the bus stop. Sometimes I lose myself in his eyes across the classroom or the lunch area — or even in my thoughts. Sometimes I think that maybe Billy and I will get back together, if we are really meant to be. Regardless of what may happen in the future, I learned a serious lesson through Billy. I learned that love doesn't mean losing oneself.

Rebecca Woolf

Let It Go

And the day came when the risk it took to remain tight inside the bud was more painful than the risk it took to blossom.

Anaïs Nin

Let It Go

Throughout your life you will be faced with the challenge of letting go. You may have to let go of a pet that has to be put to sleep, a friend who has moved to another state, or even your favorite shirt that's been shrunk in the dryer. No matter how big or small your loss might be, letting go is never easy. Your ability to let go is like a muscle you must develop. The more you practice, the stronger it gets.

It's important to understand exactly what it means to let go. If your best friend moves far away, you must let go of your attachment to living close to her. You have to learn to be okay with the fact that you won't be going to the mall together every weekend, walking to school side by side, or sitting together at lunch. However, you don't have to let go of your love for her, and you don't have to let go of your friendship. You only have to accept that the things you do together as friends are going to be different now. Letting go is the willingness to accept change and loss.

Understanding the difference between love and attachment is very helpful when a romantic relationship ends. At first everything that reminds you of him — the song you danced to at the prom, the food you used to eat together, the places you used to go. You feel like crying whenever you think of him. The only explanation you can think of for how strongly you feel is that maybe you're still in love with him.

What's more likely is that you are feeling the effects of severing an *attachment*. When you let someone into your life romantically, it's like the two of you weave a blanket around yourselves. When you split up, you have to slowly let the blanket unravel. Each thread that pulls apart can feel painful, even excruciating. But the thing you want to remember is this: Although you are miserable now, you will feel better soon. This is a guarantee. You will not feel this sad forever. Just as it took time to develop an attachment to your boyfriend, it will take time to let it go.

It is also important to be able to let go of your stress. When you catch yourself worrying or obsessing over something you really can't do anything about, gently remind yourself: *This is out of my control. I am going to let it go.* This is different from ignoring your problems. You are simply letting go of the anxiety they create. A sense of peacefulness will come over you when you stop trying to control things and surrender to what *is*.

Letting go of a serious problem like an eating disorder or drug addiction is extremely challenging. It can take a long time before you realize you even *have* a problem. It can take even longer before you realize you are ready to get over it. You may have developed the eating disorder or drug addiction as a way to cope with other painful issues in your life. It is often necessary to turn to others — people already in your life and professionals like therapists and doctors — for objective feedback and support.

Whether you are letting go of a relationship that is no longer healthy or the pain you carry due to personal problems you've endured, remind yourself that you are freeing up space in your life for new, positive experiences, people, and emotions.

Lost in the Mirror

My girlfriend and I are sitting in a fast-food restaurant, enjoying cheeseburgers, fries, and soda. Later, she'll have a chocolate sundae and I'll order a hot apple pie. A family sits beside us, children digging into kids' meals for toys and decals; across the restaurant, an elderly couple has halved a fish sandwich. We are happy to be eating here, taking it for granted. This meal, though, feels as monumental to me as winning the lottery, as walking on the moon. It also feels as unlikely.

Her name is PJ — Polly Jean, but no one has called her that since grade school — and we've been together for almost four years. We are both nineteen, in our second year of college at Miami University, which, strangely, is in Ohio. It's a lovely downtown campus with sprawling lawns, redbrick buildings, and cobblestone streets. Most of the students here are hyper-intelligent, white, beautiful, well-off, or flat-out rich. It's a cushy place. Word on campus is that one in every three young women has an eating disorder, usually anorexia nervosa or bulimia. PJ is the one in the theoretical three.

I didn't know it at first. She was the thin girl from my creative writing class whom I'd see on the treadmill at the gym; a good writer with a generous laugh and a gorgeous smile. Even when we started going out, I stayed clueless. She jogged and did aerobics in the afternoons. She ate salads with low-fat dressings, lots of steamed vegetables, unbuttered popcorn; I thought she was eating "right."

Then I noticed she got upset if her foods touched. Once she started crying after the waitress had made a mistake and served her regular dressing rather than "lite." Another time, a friend at a party told her she looked good, "like she'd finally put on some weight," and she stormed back to her apartment. For two days, she would only talk to me through the door, so I wouldn't have to look at her. She hated mirrors; she closed her eyes when she changed from her blouse to her pajama top; seeing her stomach sickened her.

It's hard to live with a person like this, harder still to be in love with her. I walked on eggshells, spoke with bated breath, worried about her, and felt guilty if I wanted a pizza. I even started counting calories, putting packages back on grocery store shelves because I thought they'd make *me* "fat." I began imagining my obesity, as PJ imagined hers. My friends applauded my eating healthier, but really healthiness had nothing to do with it.

So how did we wind up in a fast-food joint? It wasn't one thing; she didn't wake up one sunny morning and realize she was no more fat than an ant is tall. Her disorder was all about control, trying to control how the world saw, perceived, and responded to her — which, of course, is mostly out of our control. She tried to control this by controlling what she put in her body. She wanted to be accepted, to be liked and *loved*, as everyone does, and starving herself seemed a first step. I think she must have felt like a hockey player, always putting on safety equipment to protect herself from the violence of the game; by slimming down, she was ironically trying to insulate herself from the menacing world. Her disorder made perfect sense and no sense at all. Little by little, she realized the vicious cycle.

Now that we were in a steady, loving relationship, and I reminded her daily that if she looked like King Kong I'd still love her, still find her beautiful and sexy, she was able to cut herself a little slack. I'd told her this before, but now she was beginning to allow herself to believe it. She also started seeing a nutritionist and a therapist, combating — in a healthy way — her insecurities, fears, and misconceptions.

We still went through rough patches. Old habits, especially bad ones, die hard. She still avoided mirrors, and she counted calories on the sly; I'd catch her in the act and she'd feel guilty, start to cry. She had great trouble discussing her weight, and asked doctors and nurses not to say the number aloud after reading the scale. But her therapist pressed on, gently and compassionately, and slowly PJ became more comfortable with herself. One night we went to dinner and when the waiter brought our entrées, I saw that her potatoes were touching her chicken. Instinctively, I stopped the waiter and started asking him to send it back. PJ interrupted me and told him, "Actually, this is fine. My boyfriend is just a little weird about food."

I fell deeper in love with her, not because she was less of an emotional basket case or because she occasionally agreed to eat pizza, but because she started loving herself more, which, in turn, allowed me to love her as well.

So here we are, eating burgers and fries that taste great but are not exactly healthy. Though, actually, for us, they are. You cannot eat a full diet of this greasy food, but indulging every once in a while is okay. And for PJ and me, the plastic trays, dollops of mustard, and the last few fries mark a turning point in her life, in our relationship. She eats them now because she loves herself and is learning not to hang on what other people may think; she sees herself for who she is, the way I see her. Before, it was as if she were getting lost in a warped mirror, like in a carnival funhouse, where she was either tall and skinny or squat and fat. Now, when she looks at her reflection, the image is clear. She sees a healthy and smart woman, a beautiful and sexy woman, a woman who, at this moment, has a little ketchup on her chin.

Don Keys

Dear Mom

Dear Mom,

I miss you. If I could count the tears I have cried and the hours I have wished for you, the number would be mind boggling, I am sure. Sometimes it feels like I've spent my entire life without you; sometimes it feels like you are still here. But in truth, I lived 17 years with you and now, one without.

In retrospect, a year doesn't seem like a long time, but nearly everything about me is different than it was then. Life has melted back into a new kind of normal. However, I am definitely not the same person you knew.

It seems strange to say, but I am a happier person. That quote that says you can't really laugh until you can cry with your whole heart is true. My whole outlook on life has changed. You used to chide me for being such a pessimist. Well, I'm not anymore. I have discovered how to find the beautiful little things in life . . . something you taught me. Something that took me too long to learn.

You always pushed me to be my best, to take pride in my work, to reach for my dreams, and to never give up. Over the past year, I've had to learn to live without you. Gradually, I realized what you meant when you said not to let go of my hopes as we cried together on your bed. It was by no means easy, but I can now say that I have learned to love myself enough to continue on as I was before. I haven't let go of anything.

But it is time to let go of you. I'm tired of the sadness and the loneliness. It has taken me a year to understand that this is not some trial period without you. This is for real. This is forever. I am scared to death of accepting the inevitable, but I know I have no other choice.

Those who have shared your fate surround you, and I am surrounded by the people who have been in my place before — those who love me and care for me.

I trace your name with my finger one last time. This stone may not always be near me to remind me of you, but you will always be in my heart. A part of me forever.

It has taken me a year to say it, but I won't put it off anymore. Good-bye, Mom.

Sara Guilliam

Dear Bulimia

Dear Bulimia,

This is a hard letter for me to write, but I wanted to let you know that it's over between us. We have been together for a while (has it been over a year already?), and now it is time to let you go.

My friends and family told me how bad you were for me, how you never treated me right. You made me visit you in the bathroom at restaurants, wanting to get rid of whatever I ate before someone knocked on the door. You made me poke at my belly and smother my frustration in cookies and bread. You took me to the shower and made me throw up pasta and then left when I had to clean it up. You told me I was fat and worthless, too ugly for anyone but you to love.

What memories we have shared. What about the times you had me walk to exhaustion on the treadmill or made me look into the flat, brown holes where my eyes used to be? Or the times you told me I wasn't tall enough, with a smile not white enough, living for a future not bright enough. You did this to me but I stayed with you anyway. What about the day when you showed me my protruding bones? Yes, you made me fall in love with you then. I overlooked your faults.

If you are confused as to why I am ending things now, let me remind you of our fight. You saw I was very upset one day — the reason not being important — because my sadness was all you needed. You made me eat and eat and eat, and then you made my insides bleed when I tried to get rid of it. You made my best friend worry and my brother cry. You pushed me to thoughts of suicide and left me alone with the pain. Remember now?

In case you are wondering, I have found someone new, much better than you. He is around a lot more than you ever were. He doesn't leave me alone when I cry and doesn't make me visit him in the bathroom or shower. He was always there, in fact, but you were so jealous that you didn't let me truly see him. Well, I've had enough of your possessiveness.

I want back the time that I've wasted on you, the energy spent on turning my body into something you'd like. I want you to erase from my mind the look on Mom's face when she found out we were together. I need you to let go of my self-esteem and my confidence, which you've abused for so long. I'm growing back my hair, replacing the thin strands that you left me with. I know you will not miss me, since you are with millions of others. I hope they all have the courage to break up with you, too. I hope you are left alone one day, cold and friendless in your room, with no one left to bother. I wish you weren't so darn popular.

Well, I guess that's it. Please don't call anymore. You have visited me many times, and you are very desirable. Sometimes it's hard to say no to you. You came back around my nineteenth birthday, and I bet you thought we would stay together for life. But now it's really over. I know the love you had for me was only hate in disguise. I won't let you kill me, and I won't let you win me back. Take it gracefully, Bulimia. I am not your statistic anymore.

Good-bye and good riddance,
Alana

Alana Levy

Live in the Present

It is good to have an end to journey towards,
but it is the journey that matters in the end.

Ursula K. LeGuin

Live in the Present

I can't go back to yesterday, because I was a different person then.
Lewis Carroll

It is only in this moment that life can be fully lived. It is only right now that you can enjoy the sunrise or feel the cool water against your skin. Sadly, so many things go unnoticed. Instead of being in the moment, we are worrying about something we did yesterday or we are stressed about something we have to do tomorrow. Try to be aware of all the time you spend directing your attention away from the present moment.

I am afraid I will fail the test. What if I get a bad grade? What if he doesn't call? What if she tells my secret? What if they won't let me go? Why did I say that? I can't believe I did that. I feel so bad for acting that way. And on and on. As you sit and worry, life is passing you by.

I am not suggesting that you give no time or thought to what you have done and what you will do in the future. For instance, it is important to think about things you may now regret having done. But there are ways this can be accomplished constructively by focusing on what you can do *now* — in the present. If you feel bad about the way you treated a friend, think about *why* you acted the way you did. Also think about how you could have communicated or behaved in a more positive way. Don't just dwell on it. Learn what needs to be learned, apologize, and let it go. Same for the future: Do the homework, make the plans, and think about what you need to do. Just don't get caught up in obsessing over these things. The more of yourself that you are able to put into the present moment, the happier you will be.

It is impossible to stop the mind from going into the past and racing toward the future. But there are things you can do to prevent yourself from constantly worrying or stressing about what has already happened and what is yet to happen. You can remind yourself that the past can't be changed and the future can't be controlled. The only time that is truly yours is right now. In this moment, you can decide to be grateful. You can choose to be happy. When your mind starts to wander, you can continually bring yourself back to what's happening right now. This moment is where everything important exists. This moment is the only thing that is real. You really don't want to miss it.

Tricycles, Blueberries, and Crocuses

I remember my childhood like an endless walk in the park. Those lingering summers, filled with fun. Rolling in the soft grass and climbing my maple tree barefoot. Eating drippy Popsicles and huge juicy watermelons fresh from our garden. Staring in awe at the sunflowers that loomed so high above, I longed for the day when I could reach the clouds. I carelessly flew down the street on my tricycle, the strong, sure breeze on my face giving me reassurance. I knew no better getaway than the shade of our blueberry bushes. I sat in cool solitude snacking on blueberries for hours, smearing purple on my lips, and contemplating the important issues in my life. When I grow up, should I live on a tropical island or near Disney World? And what would be better to have, talking mice or a blue genie? Oh, such difficult decisions!

The fall brought trips to upstate New York for fresh cider and pumpkin doughnuts. I have long since forgotten the main purpose of those jaunts, but the traditional smell of those homemade doughnuts will stick with me for a long time. Flannel shirts with overalls come to mind when I remember the vast leaf piles that kept me busy for hours at a time.

The first snowfall always brought a frantic search for my snowsuit, as I feared the snow might melt away as quickly as it had come. Snow angels and half-finished snowmen cluttered our front yard, a sign of the creative little girl living there. Sledding and neighborhood snowball fights went on until the first crocuses came up. I was always the first to notice them. To me, they held the promise that summer was on its way, after the cherished season of yellow rain boots and splashing in mud puddles.

Now the sunflowers appear shorter and the leaf piles seem smaller. I still fly down hills on my bike, but I check for cars first. I still enjoy blueberries, but I've realized purple isn't a good lip shade for me. I now avoid the mud puddles to keep my shoes clean. I've lost my love for overalls, and my head is weighed down with problems far beyond talking mice. But my world still pauses as I take time to admire the crocus. It braves the cold and pokes through the snow when all the other flowers cower deep under the protection of the soil. It shows its elegance just as we are forgetting the beautiful bouquets of last year. The crocus holds hope for what is to come, a promise of another long, fun-filled summer on the way.

Erin Brannigan

English Peas

I ate English peas today. And you know what's unbelievable? I didn't die from gagging. I didn't pass out on the table from their horrible taste, and nothing detrimental happened to my gastrointestinal system. To tell you the truth, I actually liked them. That's how I know I'm growing up.

I can remember the days when I was younger, running from the school bus, throwing down my books, and rushing to meet friends outside. We would play for hours and hours, hoping to avoid that inevitable sunset. But the night always came, and our moms called us in, even after we'd begged for a few more minutes. Recently I sat in the chill of the evening wondering if given the opportunity I could really "play" again. And I realized that part of my life was over. I've moved on to bigger things for fun. Yet, I miss rolling down grass hills until I could hardly walk. And I miss laughing so hard that my stomach hurt as the tears rolled down my face. I miss catching lightning bugs. Yes, sometimes I miss the small things.

I found a picture of "the boy" the other day. I really thought that I loved him. From the time I was four, I had wanted to marry him. He was my first kiss, my first love, and the first one to break my heart. I remember sobbing for hours and hours and writing millions of those five-page letters that you never send.

My pain seemed unbearable and the tears eternal. Who would ever heal my shattered heart? But as I looked at that picture, faded by the hands of time, I realized that my heartache had faded as well. There really are more fish in the sea. Time eventually does heal the pain.

I looked at my mom the other day and thought of the times I've thrown myself bawling on the bed, convinced that she'd never *truly* understand. I remembered the slammed doors and the hours I attempted to give her the silent treatment. I was always the first to speak. All the fights about boys and clothes and the phone came rushing back to me. But as I thought of the person I have started to become, I realized that my mom is the woman I've always hoped to be. The arguments eventually pass, and a bond stronger than any I've ever known has begun to form. She is my new best friend.

I'm leaving for college in three months, which means leaving my boyfriend of four years (I *did* meet someone else who won my heart), my parents, and my three closest friends. It's strange, this growing-up thing. Everyone tells you not to wish any of it away. Then as soon as you understand what they mean, it's as if you are one wish too late. One minute you're longing to be sixteen, and the next moment you're dying to have sixteen back all over again. I've decided that I'll take things as slowly as I possibly can. I'm going to make as many new memories as I can fit into my heart. I'll play again; I don't think it's ever too late. Today I will tell my parents that I love them. I think I'll eat peanut butter and jelly — and save English peas for adulthood.

Amanda Bailey

Just for Today

Just for today I will hold my head high,
and forget my problems.
I can smile and make everyone else's day better,
even if behind that smile I cry.

Just for today I will walk away from a fight,
though I may feel hurt inside.
I will ignore what is said,
and continue on peacefully.

Just for today I will set an example,
when I feel the need to hurt.
I will laugh and walk away,
people will admire me more.

Just for today I will say only positive things,
I will treat others the way I would want to be treated,
instead of the way they treat me.
I will be confident that life is like a mirror,
if you smile at it, it smiles back,
and what goes around comes around,
so one day that smile will return to me.

Just for today I will stand tall,
I will not look at the ground,
but instead share happiness with others.
I will not compromise my morals,
instead I will offer opinions,
and accept reactions without question.

Just for today I will accept life's ups and downs,
and know that they only make me stronger in the end.
I will understand that doing what is right and knowing what is
    right are separate issues,
but with strength I can bring them together to make the world
    a better place.

Just for today I can.

Mollie Moir

Have Faith

If I had just one wish,
I'd visit younger days.
And tell the younger me,
"It all works out okay."

Jessica Somers

Have Faith

Sometimes even to live is an act of courage.
Seneca

Faith can mean different things to different people. My definition of faith is the belief that there is something bigger than me
running the show. Faith is the understanding that things do turn
out for the best. Faith gives you the courage to ask for help and
the security to know you will receive it.

There are many ways to strengthen your faith. One of them
is keeping a journal. By doing so you can look back and see how
difficult issues resolved themselves. A bad situation you were
in — that you thought would never get better — did. Things
you hoped and prayed for came to fruition. You might have been
heartbroken over a relationship that didn't work out, but six
months later you see that the ending of that relationship made
space for the much better one you are in now. A friend was there
for you at the moment you needed her most. You are, in fact,
making progress with a difficult problem like an eating disorder
or an emotional imbalance.

It is easy to forget how perfectly life works out. When you
are down, you believe that things never work in your favor. But
if you look back, you see that, in many cases, things happened

exactly the way they needed to. The more you pay attention to these things and take note of them, the more you build on your faith.

Having faith is a choice you make. *You* decide to believe in God, or life, or the voice that lives inside your heart. Believing in something indicates you trust life. That makes all the difference between being afraid and living fearlessly. As you grow to trust that life is often as it should be, you also begin trusting yourself. An amazing security comes from knowing that no matter what happens, you will be okay. This is the real beauty of having faith.

My Road to Happiness

Normal. What is normal? With curly red hair, olive-green eyes, and a beautiful, two-thousand-dollar smile (thanks to braces), I fit in with my senior class like a bird in a flock. I am intelligent, hardworking, polite, cheerful, and friendly. Yet, I deceive. I have secrets.

The old adage is true: Looks can be deceiving. And I should know, because I am a deceiver. What I do behind closed doors is not bad. I do not commit crimes or abuse animals. However, my actions are not normal. I have a disease called Obsessive-Compulsive Disorder.

When I was twelve years old, I knew there was something wrong with me. I could not understand the urges I felt inside my brain. Why was I so afraid of germs? Why did my handwriting have to be perfect? Why did I have to count to sixteen when walking, writing, or talking? Why was I so anxious? Why did I repeatedly spell words in my head that had an even number of letters? Why wasn't I like all the other kids?

As I got older, life became more difficult. I socialized less and less with friends. I became a recluse. I stopped eating everything but dry cereal and canned soup, and I wondered why other people didn't realize how many germs were in their food. The spelling in my head became worse. My brain's urges consumed my time

221

and energy. "Must wash hands!" my brain would shout. "Must disinfect! Must take a shower! Must count sixteen of everything!" What was happening? Was I losing complete control of my life? Was I insane? What was my problem?

Finally, my mother brought me to the pediatrician. Examining my cold extremities and listening to my slow, starving heart, the doctor asked, "Have you stopped eating?" I wanted to scream. I wanted to ask him how a person could eat when there were so many germs in the world. But I knew he wouldn't understand. *Nobody* understood what I knew. To others, germs were nothing. Oh sure, an occasional cold or the flu was annoying to them. To me, these minor illnesses meant the difference between life and death. Keeping away the germs equated to saving my life and the lives of my family members.

I didn't scream. Instead, I responded softly, "Yes, I have stopped eating."

Warmly, the doctor said, "Michelle, I believe you have anorexia. I am going to refer you to an eating disorder specialist."

An eating disorder specialist?! Sure, I thought, that's what it is. I have an eating disorder. I could live with that. When my friends wondered why I didn't eat, I could explain to them that I have anorexia. I could use the excuse that I felt fat. I could hide the secret of my paranoia with germs, unevenness, and imperfection. I was a normal teenager after all!

So my mother and I went to the hospital to see this eating disorder specialist and his team. I was weighed, and blood was drawn. The psychiatrist asked me about three questions. "So you feel fat, eh?" the older man asked, peering at me over the rims of his thick bifocals. I nodded shyly. "Do you feel depressed?" I nodded again. "Ah-hah! Why do you feel depressed?" I thought for a minute. Was I depressed? I didn't think so. "Well?" the psychiatrist asked. "My hair is ugly," was all I could manage to reply.

"Okay, I see. Now, how about if we start you on an antidepressant? It will make you feel much better," he said, smiling as if he had discovered the cure for cancer.

Do I really need this? I asked myself. I guessed it would be better if I cooperated. I didn't want him to ask about my chapped hands or the way I was tapping my foot in a sixteen-beat pattern.

After the very short visit to the specialist, my mother and I were heading home. Clutching the antidepressant in my hand, I wondered whether it would deplete me of my energy to run up the steps sixteen times, or if it would suppress my immune system.

Time pressed on. I still didn't eat much. I was told by the specialist to drink whole milk, to eat lots of meat, and to allow myself an unlimited amount of junk food. How could he be so oblivious? Didn't he realize that milk, meat, and junk food contained an enormous amount of germs?

My weight slowly dipped lower and lower. Finally, I was admitted to the locked psychiatric ward at the local hospital where my eating disorder specialist worked. The first night, I was served meat loaf. *What a stupid hospital!* I thought. *They're going to sicken all their patients with E. coli!* Of course, I refused to eat the blob of ground beef and only nibbled on a roll and some graham crackers. Another night, I was at an eating disorders support group during dinner hours. When I arrived back to the ward, my food had been sitting on the counter for over an hour. I had a fit. I refused to eat the bacteria-laden meal. They recorded on my chart: "Michelle's refusal to eat her dinner is likely related to the arrival of a new eating disorder patient to the ward."

I did eventually gain weight, mostly by drinking five milkshakes per day that were loaded with calories. At least the shakes came in a sealed can. I just wanted to get out of that torture chamber. I wanted my unlocked bathroom at home so I could wash my hands as often and as long as I pleased. And I wanted to go back to eating my safe, "germ-free" meals of dry cereal and canned soup.

At discharge, I was at a fairly healthy weight. However, my weight dropped again soon after, leading to a threat from my doctor of readmission to the hospital.

At about that time, I read in a book about Obsessive-Compulsive Disorder. I fit almost every description for the condition. Eureka! I knew my problem.

I carefully read the list of ways to cope with OCD. First, I decided I needed to turn my life over to God. Instead of focusing on germs and symmetry, I needed to focus on God's will. I went to church and prayed daily. Finally, I did it. In French class at school, I ate a crepe during a Mardi Gras celebration. Breathing heavily, my heart pumping, I asked to be excused to go to the rest room, where I spent the rest of the class period praying and crying. I waited for days to become ill and die from eating the crepe. Nothing happened. I was alive!

Gradually, I added more and more "scary" foods to my diet. Ice cream, peanut butter, and frozen lasagna slowly put some needed pounds on my frail body. I felt more energized and less anxious. I made sure to give God lots of praise for lending me some strength.

Next challenge: hand-washing. With great perseverance, I managed to control my urge to wash my hands after touching doorknobs or telephones. Of course, I always washed my hands with soap and warm water after using the bathroom, before meals, and after touching pets or garbage, but these are normal, healthy times to wash hands.

I succeeded the most with giving up my magic numbers of four and sixteen. I mean, what was I thinking? A number can't prevent death!

I'll admit, I am not completely better. I worry often about germs, I eat very few meat products, and the spelling in my brain continues. I still tend to wash my hands too often. But I am happy. No, I am not normal. I will never be normal. Not one single person out there is "normal." No one is perfect. I am who I am, and I am glad to be me. My brain may have been designed a little differently than other people's brains, but that doesn't mean that my life is doomed. If I didn't have OCD, I would never have appreciated all the wonderful things I have in my life, such as my loving family, caring friends, a warm house, a pantry full of food, and a spot reserved for me at Penn State next year. God has given us so many blessings, but to see those blessings, we must take off the shades in front of our eyes that allow us to see only the bad things. I know. I've been there.

Michelle Landis

A Butterfly's Wings

Teardrops fell from Shelly's face, as she held her mother's hand.
Sorrow filled her broken heart, as she fought to understand
Why her mom was dying, why she had to let her go.
And as her fear grew stronger, Shelly felt her panic grow.

For how would she survive without her mother guiding her
    along?
Giving words of encouragement, support to make her strong?
As Shelly started trembling, the tears continued down her cheeks,
She realized that the end was near, she'd prepared for it for
    weeks.

But now here in that moment, Shelly couldn't say good-bye.
Instead she stood there silently as her mother watched her cry.
And as if her mother read her mind, or maybe her heart,
She spoke her final words, intended to leave their mark.

"There are so many things I need to say, so many things before
    I go,
But time is of the essence, so it's important that you know . . .
That sometimes, you'll feel powerless, believing you can't win,
What others think of you will be the image you hold within.

"You'll feel you have to follow quietly, at someone else's pace,
And be the image on magazine covers, the perfect smiling face.
With the pressures to be perfect, you'll doubt yourself, and
    what you can be,
But I ask of you, dear Shelly, whenever you doubt yourself, stop
    and think of me.

"For when I look into your eyes, I see a million stars,
Shining from within, all your magic and who you are.
In your face, a flower's blossom, a starlit winter's night,
A butterfly's wings spread gracefully, without effort, taking
    flight.

"A summer breeze and sunlight, colorful leaves found in the fall,
Springtime filled with new life; in you, Shelly, I've found it all.
All in life that's remarkable, when I look at you, I see.
And if you can't believe that of yourself, then at least believe
    in me."

Shelly listened closely, as her mother's breath grew weak,
She wanted to remember every word her dying mother fought
    to speak.
"You can always make excuses, or you can make great plans,
You can bow your head in shame, or, Shelly, you can take a stand.

"And know how well deserved your place is in this world.
Be a clear example, be a mentor to every girl.
Take pride in all you are . . . a woman who is strong,
Even when you stumble, when you feel you don't belong.

"For God had a part in making you, and all that's on this earth,
And even if you don't realize it, you have tremendous worth.
For though a butterfly may seem delicate . . . fragile to the eye,
Don't you overlook the fact, it has what it takes to fly."

Shelly's mother closed her eyes; her life on Earth was gone,
But her words remained behind, giving Shelly the strength to
    carry on.
For in her mother's words, she heard a message reliable and true:
There is nothing in this world that a woman cannot do.

Though there are often times when Shelly feels weak and
    small,
And it would seem easier to give in to others, instead of
    proudly standing tall,
She finds herself thinking clearly of all the little girls on Earth
Who feel so unimportant, not aware of their own worth.

And then she hears her mother's voice, from a breeze softly
    passing by,
"Don't you overlook the fact, you have what it takes to fly."

Cheryl Costello-Forshey

Forgive Others

Forgiveness is the oil of relationships.

Josh McDowell

Forgive Others

We could all do without the day we find out someone has been spreading rumors about us. No one is thrilled to find out a friend has been flirting big-time with the guy she likes or, even worse, with her boyfriend. When these things happen, it is natural to be angry and hurt. When the hurt is fresh, you may vow that you will never forgive the person who made you sad or upset. But after some time has passed and you've had the opportunity to talk it out or let the intensity of the pain subside, it is time to think about forgiving.

Forgiveness does not mean you are saying the behavior that hurt you was okay. And it's quite possible that you might choose to end your friendship or relationship based on what happened. Some actions are unforgivable, but most aren't. Holding a grudge — clinging to the hurt and pain — will just make you feel worse. In order to completely heal, you have to forgive. Once you have forgiven, there is space inside your heart to feel more joy, more happiness, and more love.

Wildflowers

Late summer is supposed to be the best part of the year, and a time for new beginnings. It's when I go back to school and the wildflowers have grown, dotting the grass next to the sidewalk. I can hear the wind rustle the trees, which have started to turn brilliant hues, and watch the red and orange leaves fall off of them. They flutter like helicopters before they reach the ground, covering it with a collage of colors. The annual formal dance, the Fall Ball, is supposed to be a crucial moment in the adolescence of every teenage girl at my school, one of those nights when the weather is warm but breezy and the sun colors the sky pink as it sets. A night that makes everything seem right in the world, one that every girl can write about in her diary and daydream about when she's bored in class. Maybe for another girl . . . or just in my dreams.

I'm the girl who isn't allowed to wear makeup yet and whose parents can't afford fancy labels and clothes from the mall. I don't complain, though, because Mama works real hard. I'm the girl that the popular girls sneer at and the jocks ignore. I didn't try out for the school dance team, even though dance is my passion. Although I might have made it, I'm not pretty enough to fit in. My thick red hair and freckled face would look peculiar next to twelve blond heads of hair, and I would be ridiculed for dreaming out loud. My best friend, Leanne, is loyal no matter what. She helped me clean my new blouse last week after Alysha Sanchez dumped chocolate pudding all over me in the cafeteria. Everyone laughed and I turned firecracker red. I should be used to that sort of thing by now, though. My mom says to ignore what others say about me, because in the end their opinions don't matter. She tells me that as long as I love myself, no one can bring me down.

Once, some girls threw wet paper towels at me in the bathroom, then in gym class we played tennis and half of the girls used me for target practice. I wish that people would get bored of taunting me and avert their attention elsewhere. People say that high school is fun, but I haven't exactly had any new experiences that fuel me to walk through those double doors every morning. I'm just going through the motions so that I might become successful someday.

We switched lab partners in biology class. "Temporarily," our teacher told us, "while we study genetics." While my teacher slowly read down the roll, pairing people as he went, I buried my head in a book. To my astonishment, I was paired up with none other than the bodacious Bobby Fisher. More often than not, I spend the period staring at the back of his head. *Now*, I thought, *I get to stare at his face.* I melted when he smiled at me.

Together, Bobby and I made a pretty good team. He's always been known as a slacker academically, but with me he went above and beyond. We set the pace for the rest of the class on test scores. After two weeks, he was still as nice to me as he had been on the first day. To my utter amazement, he even said hello to me in the halls between classes. Sure, his friends shrugged and cut their eyes at me, but nonetheless he still spoke. Leanne couldn't believe it. Mama was almost happier for me than I was for myself. When I told her, she beamed for about five minutes. She knew how much this meant to me. For the first time ever, home sweet high school didn't suck as much as I had previously thought.

After we had completed our work one day, Bobby turned toward me and fidgeted with his black Uniball pen for so long that he scared me.

"Are you going to the Fall Ball, Rayel?" he asked.

"Well, no . . ." I said in a low tone.

"Really? Because I was kinda wonderin' . . . if you didn't have any plans that is . . . if you . . . well . . . maybe we could sorta go together. Um, will you go with me?" I had never believed that anyone would ever ask me out, so I hadn't rehearsed what my reaction would be when the time came.

With limited time to think, all I came up with was, "I think that would be fun, Bobby . . ." I silently prayed that he wasn't about to take back the invitation. He smiled broadly.

Leanne was as excited as I was when I told her, and Mama said she would buy me a new dress and shoes, even though I know she can't afford them. Karissa, my older sister, said she would do my hair with flowers woven in and let me borrow her makeup. (Mama said that's OK because it's a special occasion.) We don't have a camera, so Mama bought a disposable to take pictures before the dance. She says that making memories is important because pictures capture moments forever.

I am supposed to wear a long silky white dress that shimmers in the light and strappy white satin shoes that make me almost as tall as Bobby, but not quite. In my dreams, Bobby looks handsome in his black tuxedo. He wears a red shirt underneath because that is his favorite color, and I tell him he looks good in it. He wears a white boutonniere to match my white corsage. When my corsage dries out, I put it in my purse and spin around the floor, dancing the night away. The next day I take the corsage back out of my purse and tape it inside my journal. My grandma Pat has always said that mementos make the best memories. But I won't have them to show her this year, nor will I be at the Fall Ball at all.

The Wednesday after the best day of my life, I woke up sick and we thought it was the flu, but when I went to the clinic Dr. Kobernick said I had mono. My mother told Mrs. Heeley next door, who told her daughter Lisa, who told the entire school. Mono is also known as the kissing disease. Now not only does everyone think I'm a geek, I'm also now officially a slut — even though mononucleosis can be contracted through swimming pools, which is where I think I got it. People are so ignorant. I'm not going anywhere for weeks and my Fall Ball dreams have been trashed entirely.

My sickness bothers me, for it is keeping me down when I long so badly to be up. Mother Nature has planted every lush green plant as well as every spiky crisp blade of grass that grows in my yard, which I can see from my bedroom window. The sunflowers glisten in the sun, and it rains so that the wildflowers will grow. The breezes ripple through the sunny skies and paint a rainbow in them afterward. So why, when it comes to me, are things so not perfect?

Bobby apparently was susceptible to the rumor. And there I was, foolishly thinking that he was a gentleman, real and genuine. He didn't really ask about me once I was gone, but after a while he heard the rumors. Leanne told me that she walked by his table at lunch and some of the football players were joking about my illness and how I contracted it, making crude remarks. Bobby never said anything in my defense. Dreams don't turn to gold, and I should know that. Especially since Karissa always says, "If it looks and seems too good to be true, then it probably is." If Bobby were really interested in me, he would have called by now instead of listening to vicious rumors and lies. For the first time, I am truly feeling the sting of those growing pains that Grandma Pat always talks about.

From my bedroom window I can see Bobby walking a girl named Carolyn home. He gives her a handful of wildflowers that he picked from a field a couple of miles away. We call it "the meadow" because it has grassy plains that stretch for a few blocks. It looks like something out of *Little House on the Prairie*. It's beautiful in the meadow this time of year, and I remember that Bobby and I were there just a few days ago when he walked me home from school. We stopped and watched swarms of bees buzz from flower to flower, laboring in the honey industry. Bobby picked a long-stemmed purple wildflower for me and I put it in my hair. I still have it. Now, as I sit here watching Bobby and Carolyn, thinking about how I felt when Leanne told me that Bobby was taking Carolyn to the Fall Ball, envy and jealously grow inside, expanding like balloons, until they feel like they will explode. Tears fill my eyes.

My mom is a good therapist. She told me about something similar to this that happened to her in high school. "Bobby will probably drop Carolyn in a few days, just as fast as he dropped you, honey, and she won't even be sick!" I appreciated her attempt to make me feel better. I know that she is right when she says that everything will turn out okay in the end, and that I need to concentrate on loving myself more. She also says that everything happens for a reason, but I don't see the reason just yet. I don't know why I like Bobby so much anyway, and who cares if he gives Carolyn stupid flowers? I should just forgive Bobby, I know. Late summer is supposed to be the best part of the year, but I have an empty feeling in my stomach.

My sister's cute friend just came over, the one that always smiles at me, and I can hear him ask about me from the living room.

"How is Rayel? I brought over my Creed CD for her to borrow and a pack of Skittles because I remembered she likes them." He's only a year older than me. I glance toward the window and then look at my calendar. I smile because the wildflowers will be in bloom for a few more weeks.

Ebony Davis

Forgive Yourself

It is in the forgiveness of our mistakes that we are healed of them.

Marianne Williamson

Forgive Yourself

We seldom think about forgiving ourselves, but it is an important step in loving ourselves. You probably aren't aware that there are things you haven't forgiven yourself for, but if you think about it, you may find that there are. Right now there are probably a couple of things that you feel guilty, ashamed, or angry at yourself about.

So how do you go about forgiving yourself? Basically the same way you forgive someone else. Start by getting in touch with what it is you feel bad about. Try to understand why you did what you did and what your intentions were. More often than not, you will find that your intentions weren't bad; you just made a mistake or used poor judgment.

If you have done something that endangered your well-being or the well-being of others, it is still important to forgive yourself. Forgiveness is not the same as saying it was okay to do something you now know was wrong. You aren't condoning your behavior; you are simply forgiving yourself for the poor judgment that led you to it. Try to learn something from your mistake, allow yourself to feel the pain it caused, and decide not to do it again. If you need help preventing yourself from engaging in dangerous behavior again, talk to an adult you trust to find out the best way to get assistance. Once you have gone through the process of forgiving yourself, then it is time to move on.

Picking up the Pieces

I struggled for weeks, desperately trying to be the legs on which our tottering relationship was balancing. But, eventually, everything toppled over and all I could do was just stand staring, overcome with shock and anguish, yet too exhausted to pick up the pieces. I *could* have blamed it on him. He had betrayed my trust one too many times. He was too lazy and immature. Or I *could* have blamed it on myself. I was too committed and overprotective. But the more I thought about it, the more I realized that our relationship was strangely similar to the game where you stack narrow blocks of wood on top of one another in rows of three. Everything started out solid and sturdy, but as the months progressed, pieces of the whole were withdrawn until the shaky structure crumbled to the ground in a heap of hurt feelings, angry tears, and painful memories.

The day "us" ended haunted my mind for weeks. I *thought* I could read every look on his face, but that day he wore an expression completely unfamiliar to me. I asked him what was wrong, but deep inside I knew what he was going to say. His eyes pleaded with mine and I remember slowly taking off the jacket he had lent me earlier that day. I pressed it to my cheek, breathed in the familiar scent, and handed it to him while silent tears began to flood my eyes. He brushed one aside with his finger and walked away without a single word. I remember looking down at my outcast arms that hung in the frozen air, empty and bare without a soul to reach out to. There weren't any strong arms to hold me, and there wasn't a soothing voice to subdue my pain.

Alexander Graham Bell once said, "When one door closes, another opens. But we often look so regretfully on the closed door that we don't see the one that has opened for us." It took me months to avert my eyes from the door that had been slammed in my face. I stood looking through the keyhole at him living his own life. A life that didn't involve me. I banged on the door, I kicked and screamed till I was dizzy, but all I could do was stand outside, looking in.

One day I began to realize that in the midst of all my pain, I had neglected everything that was once important to me. I found myself standing there friendless, my family completely shoved away, and several months of my youth wasted on a foolish, teenage boy. A wave of relaxation washed over me, and I knew then and there that I was going to be my own person and rely on no one but myself for my happiness. I was going to forgive myself for past mistakes and start over. Today I would begin to live my *own* life no matter who decided to slam their door in my face. Relationships are always collapsing, but only the strong can pick up the pieces and rebuild their lives using their experiences as footholds the next time around.

Emily Starr

Dear Self

Dear Self,

    This is a long overdue letter, and for that I am sorry. In fact, a lot of what I want to say in this letter is about apologizing. I never made a conscious choice to hurt you. And yet I have — in so many different ways. Strangely enough, my motivation for doing most of the abusive stuff I did to you was about trying to make me — us — feel better.

    From as far back as I remember, I never felt completely normal, or at least what I thought was normal. I would look at other girls and they just seemed better, smarter, and basically more together. I realize now that we all struggle and probably all feel like everyone else is more blessed with something that we didn't get.

    I am sorry for the way I have treated you. I am sorry for the things I have said and for the complete lack of faith I have had in you at times. I apologize for not regarding you in the way you deserve, and most of all for not placing your needs above all others. I have looked everywhere but to you for the love I need. I have done things and acted in ways that are shameful, all in the name of earning someone else's love, when all the time there you were just waiting for me to look inward.

    I know you know that our journey will be a long one, and it will be far from easy. I am afraid that I will fail again, and there is a voice that speaks loudly warning me to not even try; that I am only asking for disappointment. But you deserve a hundred more attempts at getting it right and if that is what it takes, well then, a hundred more it will be.

I know, as you do, that the journey will be filled with steps forward, followed by steps back. But that is okay. Each day I will wake up with a renewed effort and a humble prayer for the guidance I need to get back to you and to the spirit that is truly me.

I know you forgive me and I am so grateful for that. Today is a new day and, with your love and support, I will take those small, but very important, steps forward.

I really do love you,

Me

Ask for What You Need

*We human beings can survive the most difficult of circumstances
if we are not forced to stand alone.*

James Dobson

Ask for What You Need

We are one, after all, you and I, together we suffer,
together exist, and forever will re-create each other.
Teilhard de Chardin

If I have to ask for it, then I don't want it. How many times have
you felt this way? How many times have you wanted others to
figure out what you need and then give it to you? And how many
times have you been angry or hurt because they didn't?

When you were a baby, you cried when you needed food,
physical care, or attention. You weren't shy about letting people
know you needed something. If they didn't hear you the first
time, you just cried louder. Wouldn't it be absurd if babies just
laid there and thought, *Well, if my mom can't figure out that I need
to be held, then forget it. I don't want her to hold me anyway.* And
instead of crying louder, they thought, *I can't believe my mom
doesn't know it's time to feed me. She must not love me anymore.* This
sounds funny but if you pay attention, you may see that you actually think this way sometimes.

You want your significant other to be a mind reader. You
think, *It isn't romantic if I have to ask,* or *If he really loved me, then
he would know what I want.* Guys, as well as friends, parents, siblings, and the rest of the world, don't always magically know

what you need. Expecting others to always be aware of your needs is unfair.

Think about your friends, for instance. Do you have a friend who is just a little oversensitive and you feel like you have to be extra careful when you are around her? Does she expect you to anticipate and meet her needs, and does she get mad at you if you don't? This can be a drag. After a while, you don't really want to hang out with her very much. Try to keep this example in mind when you are afraid to speak up and let others know what you need. It is easier to be with someone who tells you when she needs something or if something is bothering her, than to be with someone who wants you to guess what she is thinking.

Part of loving yourself is asking for what you need. This can mean many things. It can mean asking for a snack when you're hungry, asking someone to stop teasing you if your feelings are getting hurt, or asking for help with a serious problem that's gotten too big for you to handle on your own. Feel confident and secure enough to trust that your needs are valid and that it is okay to let others know what they are. Asking doesn't always mean you will get what you want, but it certainly increases the chances.

Hopeless

I'm all alone in a room that's dark,
Fighting the urge to add another mark.
My tears are flowing, my thoughts collide,
And the end result I'll have to hide.

I'm battered, bruised, and all alone,
Unable to fight this on my own.
Friends used to help me through the day,
But they saw my pain and ran away.

I'm growing weaker as the days pass,
Afraid today might be my last.
I know the next move is up to me,
Asking for help is the only key.

Rene Gardner

Silent Screams and Secret Scars

I sunk painfully deeper into my bed. Another horrible day and I felt empty inside. I locked my door, opened my dresser, and pulled out my weapon of choice. I kept it wrapped in a piece of white cloth.

A voice inside my head screamed at me, *Don't do this to yourself, Kristen!*

I shakily unwrapped my weapon and ran my finger over the cold blade. The voiced raged on: *Kristen, stop it! You are so stupid. You have no self-control, you idiot!*

With teary eyes and blurry thoughts, I pulled up the sleeve of my shirt, revealing all the scars from the other "bad days." I wiped all thoughts from my mind, and with one quick swipe I cut my flesh. I watched with relief as the crimson beads began to surface. Acidic tears streamed down my face, burning into the colorless flesh of my cheeks.

You're so stupid! the voice inside my head screamed. *Look what you did. How are you going to hide this? Huh? You stupid loser.*

I ignored the pain and settled myself into bed. Without warning, something clicked inside me. It was so clear. I knew that tomorrow I was going to do something different. I was going to do the most responsible thing I had ever done. I was going to tell somebody.

The next day I did exactly that. With a throbbing arm I went to school, prepared to expose two years' worth of self-destructive behavior to a teacher I trusted.

My head went foggy as I exposed my secret sin. I revealed the fresh scar, dripping with memories from the night before. I explained how for the last two years I had found relief in cutting myself. Watching the scarlet blood was like watching the pain wash away from my body.

When it was all over, years' worth of emotions and bad memories were floating in the air, untethered. My teacher looked me in the eyes and hugged me. She told me that she understood what I was going through, and that she would help me get the help I needed.

That night I went back to my room and sank, once again, into my bed and began to cry. But this time I was crying tears of relief, not despair.

That day my self-responsibility kicked in. It was okay to ask for help. It was okay to admit I couldn't handle it by myself. I am slowly getting better, and I have come to realize something. People have an extraordinary power to either hurt or heal themselves. Now it is up to me to continue to choose healing.

Kristen Peterson

I Need Help

The image of a frail, delicate teenage girl appears before me. Her high, hollow cheekbones and wavy, blond hair scream out "classic beauty," while her brown eyes pierce me with their vast intelligence. But her face is gaunt, dark, and emaciated, with sullen eyes that possess sadness so desperate that its voracity is unknown to most. Yet something is uncannily familiar to me about this girl, as if I once knew her well. Then, I come to the realization that this confused young woman before me is none other than my own reflection, evidence of months of near-starvation that have propelled me into this low point of self-deprecation in my seemingly endless downward spiral called anorexia.

Right from the start I had been able to recognize something was wrong, that my obsession with food had grown exceedingly abnormal. My inherent ability to observe aspects of myself from almost a third-person perspective had proved to be a blessing in this particular battle. This skill had allowed me to step outside of my being and notice that I was extremely unhappy, and my not eating was just a symptom of the constant state of depression I was in.

Only a few months ago I had been a fun-loving, happy adolescent of average weight, not the least bit fat. Now, I shudder as I look in the mirror at the pile of melancholy bones that I have become. I cannot allow myself to dig deeper into this murky ditch of dejectedness. I will stand up to this sickness, this unhappiness that has sucked all life and vigor out of me, and I will conquer it. I know that I can beat anorexia; I've always been able to conquer anything I put my mind to. Now that I can admit my problem and have the desire to overcome it, the next step is to ask for help, which will lend a harsh blow to my independent nature. I know that requesting help from my loved ones is an urgent necessity in order to begin my undoubtedly rough future battle against darkness.

I silently watch my mother as she reads a book. She notices me standing in the doorway and glances up questioningly. "Mommy," I say, choking back the tears. "I need help." Despite the way in which these words run contrary to my extreme pride, a cool wave of hope envelops me and whisks me away in a salty sea of optimism toward the road to recovery.

Amie Sugarman

Letters of Despair

Meredith,

It is 11:00 P.M. on Thursday and I can't fall asleep. I've been crying and hurting and praying all night.

Tonight I went overboard. I know I did. My arm is bleeding and hurts even when I don't move it. I reinjured old wounds and dug new ones into the back of my wrist. My hand is cold and falling asleep, and my shirt is getting stained because the blood is seeping through.

I'm thirsty and sweating, tired and very much awake at the same time. What I really want to do is take something and smash it really hard. Or call someone. I guess I could call a hotline or something, but that brings me to my next point.

My parents. I don't want you to tell them. I don't want our guidance counselor to tell them. They're going to find out anyway because my shirt is bloody and my mom does the laundry. And don't worry; I know I need to tell them. But I can't yet.

I know you're my friend. I know you'll understand. At least I hope you will. You're really the only person I can tell this to.

Just about an hour ago I was dandy. I did my math homework and sat myself down to listen to shout-outs on 92.1. Then, just like clockwork, I grabbed the stuff I use and began ripping myself up. I don't feel like going into detail — but I feel like talking, if that's okay.

I'm not crying anymore. Right now I feel pure anger at and hatred for myself. And fear. Meredith, I'm scared.

Not scared enough to go running to Mommy and Daddy. I'm scared of being alone. Scared of hurting others. Scared of living and scared of dying. Scared of failing and scared of succeeding.

I'm even scared to be telling you this. Please don't breathe a word of this to another soul.

Meredith, I'm sorry to be dumping on you. I should probably stop. You have your own life, and a pretty complex and busy one at that. You don't need my problems, too.

But oh, don't you see? I can't tell these feelings to anyone else. I won't listen to what anyone else has to say about it. I hate to put more pressure on you; you deal with a lot already. But, Mer, you are my only hope right now.

Sara

Sara,

Thank you so much for telling me. You can tell me anything, anytime, because I completely understand. I will always have time for you. My life would be nothing if you weren't in it. I will help you as much as I can. I won't tell your parents, but if you don't tell them soon, I will have to tell someone. I am going to be home this weekend, and if you need to call me, feel free. I am very scared for you, and I will help you get through it — but you have to want to. You and I need to hang out this weekend — at least to go to a movie or something. Every time I see your arms, I just want to cry and make you all better, but I can't do that unless you want the help. I hate how you put on an act at school, but I know you have to do it. Just remember that I am your friend and I don't want to lose you. So, please, let me help you. I love you so much. Please, let me help. You are not alone. I am in it forever.

Meredith

Meredith,

I'm sorry I've hurt you. I don't mean to, I don't want to, and I don't have to. But in a way, I must. This is scary for me, too.

I can't hide behind long sleeves and Band-Aids forever. I will have scars that won't go away. Can't you just see me going out on a date or something and not being able to wear short sleeves? And the dance . . . the top I have has three-quarter-length sleeves. I probably won't be able to wear it.

Cutting is so easy. When I do it, it's all I think about. And after I do it, it's all I think about. I can't stop thinking about it. That's what's so great about it . . . I concentrate on it alone. It's heavenly.

Then, I break down. I look at my arm and wash the blood off with cold water. The redness and the imprints won't go away, though. They stay. When I go to sleep, my arm is so sore I can't move it without it stinging. I don't fall asleep until very, very late and I wake up fifteen minutes before my bus comes. My parents stare at me while I eat breakfast, I do a few chores, and have only about nine minutes to get dressed and do makeup and stuff. I come to school looking and feeling like a total mess, but I put on a smile, and a positive attitude. I present myself like a healthy person. I'm not — but hopefully someday soon I will be.

Sara

Meredith Wieck

Look Within

Enter eagerly into the treasure house that is within you,
and you will see the things that are in heaven;
for there is but one single entry to them both.

Isaac the Syrian

Look Within

Most of the qualities that make me beautiful aren't visible. I'm
beautiful for what's on the inside. I don't have a perfect shape.
I don't have the face of a movie star. Actually, I have the face
of a thirteen-year-old girl, pimples and all. But when I'm
trying to make myself look physically pretty and beautiful,
I use my personality.
Stephanie Hoehn

Have you ever been friends with someone you hadn't met face-
to-face? Perhaps someone you got to know over the Internet, or
a pen pal? When you finally meet her, you are amazed at how
different she looks from what you had imagined. Who we are on
the outside is sometimes very different from who we are on the
inside. And as you have heard many times, what is most important is who you are on the inside. Looks change as you get older,
and what is beautiful to one person might not be beautiful to another. Unless you walk around all the time holding a mirror in
your hand, what you look like is not the part of yourself that you
live with the most. The essence of who you are exists in your
heart and in your mind. That is the part of you that controls
whether you have a good day or a bad day. It is the core of who
you are.

Look Within

When you find yourself feeling sad, unloved, or unpopular, take a moment and think about yourself exclusive of anyone else's thoughts or opinions. What matters to you? What do you like about yourself? What is special about you?

Instead of looking to the outside to make you feel better, think about what you can do to soothe yourself on the inside. Look within, and you will find the love you need.

My Best Feature

I asked my friend this afternoon,
As I gazed into my reflection,
What she thought of what I saw.
She said, "Images are usually misconceptions."

I started to put down my appearance,
Wishing I was thinner or taller.
She looked at me with understanding eyes,
Saying, "Superficial wishes only make you smaller."

I knew she was right, but who was she to talk,
For she was every guy's dream.
I tried to point this out to her,
She replied, "Appearances aren't always what they seem."

"Tell me five features you admire in yourself," she said,
And I knew my troubles had just begun,
For I could see the hurt in her expression,
When I couldn't think of one.

I could not think of a single feature I liked,
And my stomach slowly started to sink.

So I turned to my friend and simply said,
"Well, what do *you* think?"

"I think you're looking at it all wrong," she said,
"And I wish I could make it clearer.
It's what's inside that makes you beautiful,
And not what can be seen in the mirror."

She said, "You're the most loving person I know,
And I hate to watch you fall apart.
If you want to know what makes you beautiful,
Your best feature is your heart."

Sara Nachtman

Pretty Much?

I go to extreme measures in my quest to look pretty. I make sure that I get the latest copy of teen magazines to stay up on my fashion savvy. I take myself cosmetics shopping to snag new items. I'm the type who tries just about any product on the market for the sake of beauty. I usually feel pretty — until I go to the powder room and inevitably run into that "much prettier girl." I look in the mirror and compare our endowments. The last girl I compared myself to looked impeccable with her tall, willowy figure, creamy skin, and expressive eyes, in contrast to my short stature, pasty skin, and plain eyes. I felt like an ugly duckling next to her. It only took a few seconds of insecure glances at her beauty to make myself feel unpretty. I walked out of the room feeling vulnerable.

I've focused so much on making myself physically beautiful that I've become oblivious to what's essential. Just as a concealer can never fill in craters, external beautification can't quite cover up deep-seated insecurities. All the makeup in the world can never make up for my poor self-image.

My feeble attempt to acquire movie star panache began by studying film heroines. I had taken to patterning my personality after Alicia Silverstone in *Clueless* or Cameron Diaz in *There's Something About Mary*. Having finally observed those characters

267

long enough, it occurred to me that both of them possess an undeniable self-assurance. Being comfortable in their own skin is what makes these actresses so gorgeous. By not paying too much attention to what others think and by being themselves, they make self-consciousness look so last-season. Oprah Winfrey recently asked her audience on one of her shows, "If you don't think you're gorgeous, how do you expect everybody else to think so?" In that moment I understood that falling in love with one's self is the first step toward a healthy self-image. I'm not kidding myself. I know I have a long way to go. But I feel better now at least knowing where to begin.

The beauty experts know that one looks good if one *feels* good. Achieving true beauty is improving what's on the inside. And nothing makes me feel as radiant as genuine happiness. What I've learned is that happiness, for me, is not in the compliments I receive or the number of friends I have, but in how I've managed to touch other people's lives. Compassion without expectation of anything in return is my recipe for the beauty mask of the soul. This beauty bounty comes as free as the makeup testers I use at the cosmetic counters. And the good thing is it cannot be wiped away. It stays with me forever.

Finesse Angelica F. Evangelista

Shadow

And as my feet hit this concrete,
and I walk upon this pavement
that I've walked upon for so many years,
I see her shadow.

I gaze up to the sky,
and I see her face in the stars.
She looks down at me, and smiles.
I feel her embrace in the warmth of
the honey golden sun.

She whispers to me within the wind
of her sorrows,
of her pains —
her heart, once weak and shattered.

Then she kisses me with soft rain
upon my lips,
and hushes my cries.

She gives me hope —
I see her in the silver glow of the midnight
moon, and I feel her strength.

I look inside her soul,
and find a treasure within
the silhouette of a girl.

That girl is me.

Bridget N. Kevin

From the Inside Out

I wasn't allowed to wear much makeup. But I thought my skin tone was uneven and I had circles under my eyes, so I begged my mother for foundation. When she finally caved in, I wore it to school with pride.

A few weeks later, I heard that going to sleep without taking off your foundation would clog your pores. Pimples? I didn't want pimples! So I borrowed my sister's makeup remover towelettes that evening as preemptive damage control.

I was astonished to see that at the end of the day, hardly any makeup came off. I wiped harder. Still nothing. Most of the makeup had worn off already. But I still looked good! How could that be?

It was then that I realized that the makeup had given me self-confidence, something I had needed badly. Because of that confidence, even without makeup, I shone from the inside out.

I still wore the foundation the next day. But I knew that no matter how uneven my skin tone seemed to me or how tired I looked, when I smiled the smile of pride, confidence, or just plain happiness, I would look good. I would be lit up from the inside out. Feeling good about yourself makes you the most beautiful person alive.

Zahava Stadler

Mirror

She stood crying in front of the mirror. Her mascara had long since smeared all over her too pale cheeks, and the mirror seemed to cruelly reflect each smudge. The dress she was wearing was a little too small, its color a little too faded, and the mirror found delight in throwing these details in her melancholy face. The longer she looked, the more details the mirror pointed out. For instance, her thin hair hung lax on her shoulders. It was a rather plain color, not very interesting. And her nylons did have a somewhat noticeable run near her knee. Sadly, she stared at the mirror's reflection, and it made her tears flow in currents, washing away the last of her black eye makeup as well as the last of her self-respect.

Then, something unusual happened, something she couldn't explain. She stopped caring. Turning away from the wretched silver surface that had ruled her life for so long, she looked inward instead. It wasn't easy. On her way to her real self, she came across many obstacles, like her weight or her clothes or even her toothy smile; these things had been so important before, but now she realized they simply stood in her way. So she dug deeper, into the part of her that had been invisible for all these years — because she had chosen not to look at it. Under the many "problems" that her mirror caused her to obsess over, there was an intelligent girl with a friendly attitude and a positive out-look. Before she knew it, her tears had cleansed her face, and her mind had cleansed her soul.

She turned back to the mirror, but this time it threw nothing in her face. She had nothing to hide and nothing for the petty mirror to laugh at. She walked toward the mirror and did something she had done plenty of times before but never really meant. She smiled. She smiled so brightly, and she was proud of every shiny white tooth the mirror reflected back to her. Then, with nothing further to say to the worthless opinions of the smooth glass on her wall, she turned and walked out, head held higher than ever before. And although she didn't notice it, the mirror itself had changed. A tiny crack had etched its way across the mirror's once flawless surface . . . almost like the scar of a battle lost. She had finally won herself back.

Rachel Hislop

The Beauty of Me

I'd like to think that my personality makes me beautiful. I mean, some people say that my outer appearance is nice, but my personality makes it even better. If you think about it, when you like somebody, you tend to like their personality and not just their looks.

What I like about my personality is that I try to be a friend to everyone and not make judgments. It can be hard, though. Another thing I find that makes me beautiful is that I stay positive before I meet someone. For instance, before meeting someone new I tell myself, "I will like this person," and I usually do. I also love to be with my friends and family. They are a big part of my life and I think that being with them and getting all the love that they give me makes me even more beautiful.

My mom has always said, "A beautiful person is someone who is happy with herself and loves the person she is." I think that is so true, because if you are truly happy with yourself and you also love who you are, then you really do feel beautiful. I know this firsthand. I used to be very unhappy with myself and I always felt depressed, stressed out, and not good enough. For one, I thought I weighed too much and I thought I looked fat. Then I realized that I should just be happy with the way I am. It worked! I really did start to feel less stressed out, not depressed at all, and I didn't even think about being good enough anymore. Best of all, I truly felt beautiful.

I mean, I know I'm not perfect, but I think that being a more positive person is what really makes me beautiful.

Lauren Fischer

It's the Inside That Counts

Once upon a time, not too long ago,
There lived an old man by the name of Joe.

Joe made dolls of all shapes and sizes.
Some wore coats and some wore disguises.

They ranged in colors from black to white,
And came in all sizes from heavy to light.

There were some that were simple and some could light up,
Others would talk and never shut up.

Each doll was different, no two were the same,
And every doll had its own name.

Roger resembled a star football player,
And William looked a lot like the mayor.

Bertha was short, a bit round and quite plain,
While Jenny was pretty and destined for fame.

Joe sold the dolls in a small, redbrick store,
Twelve hours a day people came through the door.

Folks bought the dolls for kids, sisters, and brothers.
Needless to say, some sold better than others.

The boys liked the ones
That held knives and ray guns.

A doll with long hair and a long, puffy dress,
Is usually the one that the girls liked the best.

Some people collected one of each kind.
Others had one special figure in mind.

One day a girl, who was unlike the rest,
Came in to pick out the doll she liked best.

She would randomly pick out a doll from the pile,
Keeping her eyes closed, she would hold it a while.

Then ever so careful, she'd put that doll back,
And pick up another doll from the rack.

Joe watched the girl as she held Annie, then Nick,
Secretly wondering which doll she would pick.

Then she picked up a doll no one handled before,
Not noticing the face or the clothes that it wore.

The doll had loose seams and was missing a leg,
And the clothes that it wore were made out of a rag.

The hair on the doll was like the hair of a clown,
And the face of the doll bore an unpleasant frown.

This doll was about as worn out as they came.
It was the only doll that didn't have a name.

But as the girl held it, she knew with no doubt,
That this was the doll she'd been dreaming about.

Joe rang up the doll and when he was done,
The total came to $3.71.

As she gave him the money she said, "It's too bad,
The doll that I want has a face that's so sad."

"What made you pick her? She looks such a dread.
Why didn't you choose one with a smile instead?"

The girl looked up at Joe and said, "I just bet,
I know why this doll is so very upset.

She sat on the shelf being the best she could be,
But an ugly old doll was all people would see.

Since no one would hold her, they never found out,
It's not the outside, but the inside that counts."

Joe was impressed by this little girl,
She's one of those people who sees a rock as a pearl.

She was unlike the rest and what set her apart,
Was instead of her eyes, this girl saw with her heart.

Mollie Thill

Celebrate Yourself

How could I have been anyone other than me?

Dave Matthews

Celebrate Yourself

Taking the time to celebrate is an essential part of loving yourself. I remember working on my third book and being under a great deal of stress. Things were going very well with the first two books, and I felt a huge responsibility to make the third one even better. I was having lunch with a friend and she asked me, "Did you ever take the time to celebrate the success of your first two books? Have you given yourself some kind of reward for all your hard work?" I told her I didn't have time for that, but maybe I'd do it after the current book was finished. She went on to explain that without celebrating the completion and the success of the previous books, I was denying myself something I deserved. She told me I wasn't recognizing and honoring my hard work and the blessings of its success. Without doing this, she explained, I was actually making it harder to go on to the next book. It's as if you continually did nice things for someone and that person never thanked you. After a while you would start losing the impulse and the energy to continue with your generous behavior. As you practice the steps in this book and spend time learning to love yourself, it is important to take time every now and then to thank yourself. Allow yourself to feel good about your progress and to celebrate it.

When you begin to love the fact that you are different from

everyone else in some ways, or you start to consciously say nicer things to yourself, this is something to celebrate. When you are faced with a difficult decision and you make the hard but right choice, or you stretch yourself beyond what is comfortable in order to become a better person, this is cause for celebration. Just remember that when you don't take the time to say "thank you" and "nice job" to yourself, you don't have the same passion and drive to move forward and continue doing the work necessary to develop a good sense of self-worth.

Take a moment and think about how you'd like to celebrate your completion of this book. As you read it, you may have gone through changes in your attitude and outlook — some easier than others. There are elements to the 24 steps that aren't easy. You were asked to look at yourself in a new way, and that took great courage. But you did it.

I am now asking you, like my friend asked me, "Are you going to take the time to mark this moment? Are you going to reward yourself? Are you going to love yourself enough to celebrate who you are?" I hope your answer is yes.

My Hands, My Accomplices

In one bold salute, I sealed the show — our final package of music and magic. Once again, the Central Hardin Marching Band had reached the destination of a five-month journey: state competition. As my fists returned to my sides, I watched as our entourage left the field. A wild sea of emotion flooded my mind and my heart as I stared at the ground twelve feet below. With great reluctance, I descended. In a world of fantasy, I longed to mount the podium and enter my private realm of musical bliss. In reality, I knew that I would never again clasp the blue railing. The flame of my torch had been extinguished, ready to be ignited by another. In these few moments, my despair was inflicted by one appalling thought — graduation.

I stared down at my hands, clothed in the leather gloves that symbolized my field commander status. These two hands had been intently followed by my peers. Any beat or sheer movement gave silent instruction. With the skill of a professional mime, I unveiled hidden emotions buried deep within many souls. Looking even more carefully, I observed the size to which my hands had developed over my seventeen years. What a life they had endured!

These were the same tiny hands stamped at birth onto my birth certificate. They had broken jewelry, scratched skin, and pulled hair. With an impeccable grasp, they had clung to a parent, a doll, and a sacred ribbon. These hands learned to handle bottles, cups, silverware, crayons, scissors — a variety of fascinating new objects. They learned the miraculous joy of cradling a baby sister, helping her learn to walk, breaking her falls. With age, these appendages created prizewinning essays, stories, poems, and artwork. They clasped speeches, microphones, scripts, and hard-earned awards. Their muscles had cramped from endless days of intense homework and after-school practices. Through training, these hands played the ivory keys of a piano and covered the silver tone holes of a clarinet. Handshakes, hugs, applause, high-fives — they never failed to help. These were the hands soiled by volunteer, community, and school service. They brushed aside sweat and tears, determined never to rest. These were not only my hands, they were my accomplices in life.

Many have told me that change is inevitable and unavoidable. As I left the stadium, it hit me like a brick. My first dip into the pool of growing up left me searching for a fountain of youth. In frustration, I removed my gloves, now stained with tears, makeup, and dirt. Beneath this soiled surface were two hands — impeccably clean and fresh.

In life, I must remove the glitter and glamour of my childhood. Yet beneath this glove of memories, a clean slate awaits; my future lies in my hands.

Laura Beth Dennis

Flight of Freedom

I was put in a cage by my parents,
But now they have opened the door.
I know that my whole life is out there,
I'm not a kid anymore.

They tell me how they had felt,
The day that they were let free.
They say it was oh-so-exciting,
But their words aren't enough for me.

And now that day is finally here,
The world is mine to explore.
I know that when I step out there,
I cannot turn back anymore.

My first step will be purely courage,
My second will be disbelief.
My third one will be with great pride,
My fourth one will be up to me.

Andria Pragelas

Be

Overcome a fear
Laugh out loud
Break the silence
Speak to the crowd

Feel the joy
Taste the wind
Breathe the stars
Imagine

Model kindness
Wear peace
Show mercy
Act as least

Know her sadness
Heal his pain
Listen closely
Receive the same

Make a promise
Give from the heart
Take and return
End and restart

Rise from the bottom
Soar from the deep
Smile and rest
Desire and seek

Learn the secrets
Read between lines
Thirst for the truth
Look for the signs

Sing and dance
Love and live
And remember you get
Whatever you give

Sara Guilliam

Now that you're done with this book, what else can you do?

Join the *No Body's Perfect* online community of girls
Go to *www.scholastic.com* or *www.iam4teens.com* for more information on how to join the *No Body's Perfect* online girls' club. Learn more about the 24 steps, submit questions to and read answers from Kimberly Kirberger and other experts on teen issues, find out how to start your own local *No Body's Perfect* girls' club, and receive continuous support and guidance.

Form your own *No Body's Perfect* discussion group
Get together with some friends so you can share your thoughts on all you have read, written, and learned. You could meet once, or form a group that meets regularly.

Here are some topics for discussion and things you can do:

❀ Magazines, movies, and television influence how we feel about our own bodies by showing us female figures that don't exist in real life. Magazines use computers to digitally alter the images of girls and women we see.

❀ Society pressures girls and women to be too thin. You can do something about this by refusing to accept the media's opinion about the optimal female form.

❀ Saying negative things about our bodies makes us feel bad. See if you and your friends can make an agreement not to speak negatively about your bodies or your general appearance.

❀ Agree to do things together that are healthy, fun, and make you feel good.

❀ Make a list of girls' rights. The items on your list can be things like:
  - We have the right to refuse to be pressured by our parents, friends, or others to look different than we do.
  - We have the right to refuse to buy magazines that publish images of only super-skinny girls rather than girls who look like we do.
  - We have the right to love who we are.
  - We have the right to accept the fact that no body's perfect.

Write your own story
Share your stories about body-image, self-acceptance, and the search for identity with Kimberly Kirberger.

Kimberly Kirberger
I.A.M. 4 Teens, Inc.
P.O. Box 999
Pacific Palisades, California
90272

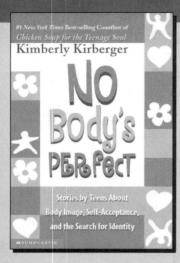